Remember
the Ladies

Remember the Ladies

21 BIOGRAPHIES AND ACTIVITIES HIGHLIGHTING CONTRIBUTIONS OF REMARKABLE WOMEN

SHERYL FEARRIEN

TATE PUBLISHING
AND ENTERPRISES, LLC

Published by Tate Publishing & Enterprises, LLC
127 E. Trade Center Terrace | Mustang, Oklahoma 73064 USA
1.888.361.9473 | www.tatepublishing.com

Tate Publishing is committed to excellence in the publishing industry. The company reflects the philosophy established by the founders, based on Psalm 68:11,

"The Lord gave the word and great was the company of those who published it."

Book design copyright © 2016 by Tate Publishing, LLC. All rights reserved.
Cover design by Joshua Rafols
Interior design by Shieldon Alcasid

Published in the United States of America
ISBN: 978-1-63418-489-2
Biography & Autobiography / Women
16.02.24

To any person who ever asked "What if?" and then acted upon fulfilling that dream!

Contents

About the Author

Sheryl Huffman Fearrien has taught multiple grades for twenty-one years. She holds a Clear California Teaching Credential for grades K-12 and a Montessori Diploma. *Remember the Ladies* began as a research project for Women's History Month, with twenty-one biographies of historical women from the past three hundred years. Sheryl used the unique contributions of each woman to design engaging activities and lesson plans that could be completed in one to two days. *Remember the Ladies* can supplement a variety of subjects—air travel, civil rights, fine arts, education, government, health/medicine, health/recreation, law, literacy, journalism, social welfare/freedom, literature, performing arts, space travel, chemistry/medicine, and physical sciences. She is also the author of two historical recipe cookbooks: *Cooking through World History* and (its sequel) *Cooking through American History*.

Sheryl and her husband, Michael, live in Northern California. The couple's three grown sons and an endearing border collie—Siberian husky mix named Chance are dear to their hearts!

Introduction

THESE LESSONS ARE designed for the novice to the most experienced teachers, as well as homeschooling parent-educators, for students from grades 6–12. The reading level is actually for students grades 9–12 reading at grade level, but the interest level is middle grades, junior high, and high school. For students grades 6–8 who are reading several years above their grade level, *Remember the Ladies* will be appropriate for them.

Contributions of women past and present have enhanced quality of life not only for their contemporaries, but also for posterity in many arenas: air travel, chemistry/medicine, civil rights, education, fine arts, government, health/medicine, health/recreation, law, literacy, journalism, social welfare/freedom, literature, performing arts, space travel, and physical sciences. Their backgrounds are varied, yet these women of integrity share several commonalities: clearly defined goals, determination and fortitude to withstand adversities and distractions, and very often supportive parents who believed gender should not restrain their daughters from achieving heartfelt dreams.

This book's focus is to profile twenty-one accomplished women and to provide one or more specific activities to engage students. Each biography has five vocabulary words (in bold print and underlined in biographies) to match with definitions and four short essay questions. As the educator, you decide how detailed the answers should be, depending on your student/s' abilities. Answer keys are included near the end of the book.

The next two pages describe Lesson Options, additional activities to further students' comprehension. *Remember the Ladies* is a valuable resource for Women's History Month as well as a supplement that can enrich most other subjects. Every effort has been made to produce factual and interesting narratives. Clear, detailed lesson plans enable educators to readily implement. I believe you and your students will enjoy my approach!

Lesson Options

Teachers, you can implement this book in various ways, choosing what works best with your students. Here are some additional options. However you use this resource, emphasis should be on involving students in their own learning, as they appreciate and enjoy the variety of contributions these accomplished ladies have given us!

1. **Daily Oral Reports**—Assign, draw names, or allow each student to choose a woman to study and then present a short oral report to class.

2. **Newspaper Articles**—Provide the biographies to students and instruct them to write Who, What, Where, When, Why, and How? newspaper articles about one or more women. Expanding on this, students could design a whole newspaper front page with pictures, maps, pretend interviews of the women, eyewitness accounts, and related articles about other happenings of the same time period.

3. **Talk Show Appearances**—Students, in twosomes or threesomes, will present information about a woman in a TV talk show format to class. One student will be the interviewer/host and one student will be the noteworthy woman guest. A third student could present a commercial for a typical product the public in that time period would likely need or want to purchase. Students will use the biographies to

formulate the interview questions and the Internet for possible time period specific commercials. This option presents great opportunities for students to use their creativity!

4. **Venn Diagrams**—As whole class, small groups, partners, or individual student assignments, (1) students will create Venn diagrams and compare/contrast two women. Where the circles overlap is the Compare section (what is *alike or similar* about the women) and the remaining sections of each circle is the Contrast section (what is *different or unique* about each woman). (2) Students could also compare a woman's life to their own life. A blank Venn diagram follows Lesson Options.

5. **Quiz Jar Review**—On small cards, put questions on the front side and answers on the back after different ladies have been studied. These can either be generated by teacher or students. It promotes more critical thinking if students help create these. A simple way would be to have students create one or two questions with answers after each biography is covered. Cards are placed in a large jar (such as the big plastic cracker or cookie tubs from wholesale/discount stores). Teacher draws out cards, reading question/s, and students volunteer answers. These cards provide fun, painless review and are good for soaking up "sponge time"—those few transitional moments just before recess, lunchtime, the next class, or at the end of the school day. Upon accumulating a preset number of points for correct answers, rewards could be earned by the class.

6. **Mobiles**—Have students create mobiles to represent the different women. There are many ways to make mobiles. One simple method is to mount descriptive words and drawings of the women and their artifacts on small colored pieces of construction paper or poster board. Using different lengths of string or yarn, hang all pieces from coat hangers. The time and complexity spent on the mobiles should be determined by taking into account the skills, abilities, and sophistication of your students.

7. **Maps**—(1) Using large world and USA wall maps, place removable dots in several colors with women's initials to indicate locations of their hometowns, states or countries, and places of accomplishments. Example: Marie Curie, Warsaw, Poland (hometown), and Paris, France (place of accomplishments). (2) Students draw own maps and indicate locations of women's origins and accomplishments.

8. **Timelines**—Make timelines spanning the years 1744 to present day. For smaller timelines, use adding machine tape. For larger timelines, use plain white shelf paper. Measure accurately and mark off each year. Mount timeline on the wall around the room. As each woman is studied, indicate her life span with colored line (yarn, crayon mark, etc.) and her accomplishments with small strips of paper. Example: Louisa May Alcott, 1832–1888 (life span), and her books such as *Little Women*, 1869, etc. (accomplishments). By using different colors, it is easy to distinguish individual women where their life spans overlap.

9. **Women of Accomplishment Museum**—Host a museum, inviting friends, family, or another class to view. Students select and display completed activities. Some students could act as curators for each woman's display. Other students may want to dress in period costumes and/or use appropriate props to represent individual women.

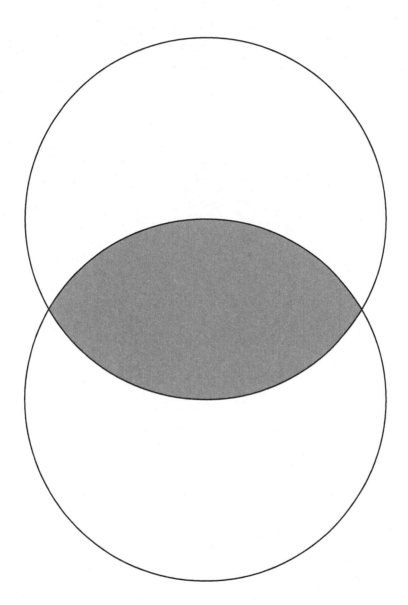

Venn diagram

Abigail Adams:
"Remember the Ladies"

ABIGAIL SMITH ADAMS was born in Weymouth, Massachusetts, on November 22, 1744 to the Reverend William and Mrs. Elizabeth Smith. She was very small and looked quite delicate. Mother and Grandmother Quincy were extremely worried that the infant would not survive long. They bundled her warmly in layers of clothing and blankets under a doeskin robe. Just before they whisked baby Abigail off to the church where her father could baptize her, Grandfather Quincy arrived. He noted that babies smaller than Abigail had survived and lived long and impressive lives. He had no doubt his little granddaughter would live—and Abigail did!

Often Abigail was not allowed to attend school due to her parents' concern for her health. She was frequently ill. A common cold could quickly turn into pneumonia. Mortality rates for pneumonia were about fifty percent. (Remember, antibiotics were not available until the twentieth century!) Precautions were taken to keep Abigail as healthy as possible. Curious Abigail thirsted for knowledge. Father had graduated from Harvard and told Abigail that her mind was a gift from God. He encouraged his daughter's learning at home and acted as her tutor. At a young age, Abigail learned to read. The books in Father's library opened other worlds to her! Often Abigail was sent just a few miles away to the home of Grandmother and Grandfather Quincy, her mother's parents. Grandfather's library was even larger than Father's! What a joy this was for Abigail!

On other occasions, Abigail was sent to her Aunt Elizabeth's home in Boston, about ten miles away. Both locations were deemed healthy environments for the child. Mother, Grandmother Quincy, and Aunt Elizabeth also made sure Abigail learned skills necessary for young ladies: embroidering, sewing, cooking, and tending the home. When Abigail was shut in at home or visiting relatives for extended periods, she learned to stay in touch by writing letters to family and friends. This not only developed her handwriting skills but also her critical thinking skills. Later during her marriage, this **correspondence** kept Abigail and her husband connected while he was away helping **establish** a new nation.

Abigail remembered two events from her childhood for the rest of her life. Both involved gunpowder. Here is the first. In small communities throughout the colonies, villages were centered around their churches. These houses of worship had been important from the founding of the colonies. They served as community meeting places and community storehouses as well as churches. They had tall steeples modeled after European churches. After all, the original colonists had come from European countries. In prerevolutionary and revolutionary days, colonists often stored their gunpowder in the church **garrets**. This was the case in Weymouth, Massachusetts. One day, Abigail was with her brother, Will, waiting for their father to finish checking the meetinghouse. A group of their friends, all boys, were engaging in musket target practice. The lads would not allow Will to participate because he was smaller and younger. They said they did not want to waste their gunpowder. To impress the boys, Will volunteered that he knew where there was much gunpowder—in the church garret—and he knew where the key was kept! The boys immediately became excited and plotted and planned to sneak into the church and take some gunpowder late that night. Abigail cautioned that this was a dangerous plan, but they ignored her warning. Abigail had no appetite for supper that evening. The boys were planning their gunpowder **escapade**, and she could not tell anyone; that would make her a tattletale. Abigail needed a secret plan to foil the boys' scheme. After her family was asleep, Abigail took Rover, the family dog, with her to the church. She planned to leave Rover in the garret to scare the boys away with his growling and scratching. Abigail knew the boys believed the rumors of ghosts haunting the garret after dark. Poor Rover had no idea why Abigail was trying to leave him alone in the garret. He kept following her as she tried to leave. Finally, Abigail heard the boys approaching! She shoved Rover into the garret and hid with him. Rover growled and scratched at the door, wanting out. Hearing this, the would-be-thieves were terrified that ghosts and the devil himself were in that garret! Completely abandoning their plan to steal gunpowder, they quickly ran home to escape the wrath of the feared beings! Abigail and Rover returned home. No one ever learned how Abigail and Rover had foiled the gunpowder theft until many years later!

Weeks later in the middle of the night, that second event occurred. Suddenly, a huge fire lit the dark sky, waking everyone in the surrounding community. Father and others rushed out to see what had happened. The church garret and steeple were on fire! Soon a mighty explosion erupted that could be seen twenty miles away! The roof had blown off the church! The fire was so huge and bright that many people came from miles around to see what had happened. Abigail's parents welcomed many people to stay the night in their home. Every nook and cranny was filled with unexpected guests! The fire eventually burned out. The boys admitted to Abigail that they were all so relieved that the ghosts had scared them away from gunpowder. Seeing the force of the fire convinced the boys they would have been killed had they been in the garret or steeple on the night of the fire.

In her teen years, Abigail met many young, educated men during stays with her grandparents and aunt Elizabeth. While her family considered various men of means as a potential future husband for their daughter, Abigail had eyes only for a young lawyer named John Adams. He was short and squat, physically very unlike the other potential suitors. Why was she attracted to him? Abigail and John had so much in common. They spent many hours together discussing current events, politics, and government. John could not believe that Abigail was so well-versed and interested in the same topics he was! She was unlike any other girl he had known. Abigail loved that John respected and valued her opinions. They had found soul mates! After several years of courting, John readied a home in Braintree for his wife-to-be. John and Abigail were married in the fall of 1764 by Abigail's father. Abigail was twenty, and John was nearly twenty-nine. Abigail was extremely proud of John. Many people respected him and sought his counsel.

As tensions between the colonies and Great Britain escalated, John was pressed to represent Massachusetts in Philadelphia at the first and second Continental Congresses, the committee for writing the Declaration of Independence, and, after war broke out, as commissioner to France. John's role was essentially that of an ambassador. The goal was to persuade France to help the American colonies in their quest to free themselves from British tyranny. France and Great Britain had been enemies for many, many years. John's goal should not be too difficult. On John's first trip to Europe in early 1778, he took along their eldest son, Johnny (John Quincy). The two returned home in August of the next year. By November, John was called back to Europe. This time he took not only twelve-year-old Johnny but also nine-year-old Charles. After two stays in Europe, John could not bear to be away from Abigail any longer. Abigail felt the same way being apart from her John. The war was over, negotiations for the peace treaty were complete, but John needed to stay awhile longer to arrange business between the new United States of America and European powers. John wrote to Abigail, begging her to come to him in the fall of 1783, saying the younger children, Charles (who had returned home on his own) and Tommy, were now old enough to stay with Abigail's sister. Their eldest child, Nabby, now eighteen, decided to accompany her mother. The thought of a long and potentially dangerous ocean voyage made Abigail apprehensive, but she wanted so desperately to be with her husband.

Mother and daughter arrived in England in the summer of 1784. While in Europe, Nabby fell in love with and married her father's secretary, Colonel William Smith. (Coincidently, Nabby's husband and maternal grandfather shared the same name.) Johnny returned home to complete his education at Harvard. Over the next few years, Abigail and John lived in Paris and then England, where John was the first American ambassador to England. Here Abigail met the queen and actually impressed the court ladies. Everyone was surprised that this American was so well-spoken and informed. Abigail was proud that she represented all the American women who had played such pivotal roles in the founding of their nation. She also enjoyed attending science lectures. These convinced her more than ever that American women must be educated!

Nabby, her husband William, and their baby daughter returned to America at about the same time as Abigail and John. Nabby's family was headed for New York on one ship while her parents were sailing for Boston on another. Upon arriving in Boston Harbor in June of 1788, the couple was surprised to see thousands of Americans, including their other children, Abigail's sister Mary, and other relatives, all along the waterfront to greet them! John and Abigail had returned to a grateful nation and now could return to their happy life in Massachusetts—or so they thought.

By the next year, 1789, George Washington, who had commanded the American war army, had been chosen to be the first president of the United States of America. John was chosen as the vice president. This meant a move for the Adams to New York City, the first capital of the new nation. Once again, Abigail was so pleased and proud of John. She supported him and tried to be the best wife of the vice president she could be! Abigail learned much from the gracious and helpful First Lady, Martha Washington. After two terms as vice president, John became the second American president. He took the oath of office in Philadelphia, the second capital city of the USA. During the last year of Adams's administration, Abigail and John moved into a new presidential palace when it was just finished enough to do so. This was in the nation's third and brand new capital city of Washington, District of Columbia, or Washington, DC, for short. The city had not actually been built yet, so the home appeared to stand out in the wilderness until the city grew around it. That grand home later became known as the White House, as it is today. When the couple moved in, plaster was still drying on the inside walls. Abigail kept the thirteen fireplaces blazing to take the chill off the damp, large house. The couple was expected to host political dinners and parties and pay for everything out of pocket. Abigail, always very frugal, saved enough money to provide food and drink for the many dinners and parties. Just one month after moving into the large residence, Abigail was a gracious dinner hostess to foreign ambassadors. Today, the president is still expected to host many lavish events at the White House. No longer does the money come out of pocket. Taxpayers' money covers all the costs.

Thomas Jefferson, who had been a good friend to both John and Abigail, won the presidency when John had hoped to win a second term. Bad feelings strained and spoiled their long friendship. John and Abigail were upset by the criticism of John that Thomas expressed in newspaper articles. (Before radio, television, and the Internet, this was how opinions—and in particular, political opinions—were made public.) Thomas and John now had evolved different ideas about the correct way to ensure America's future through government. While Abigail and Thomas had frequently corresponded, she stopped altogether. Abigail felt Thomas had betrayed their friendship. It was not until 1804, when Abigail learned of the death of Thomas' twenty-five-year-old daughter, that she again wrote to him. This time it was to offer condolences. The two old friends began corresponding and continued until Abigail's death in 1818.

Abigail lived seventy-four years and enjoyed a happy fifty-four-year marriage to her dear soul mate, John. While the couple spent years apart, their bond was always strong. She and John had six children: Abigail (Nabby) born in 1765, John Quincy (Johnny) in 1767, Grace Susanna in 1768 who lived just past her second birthday, Charles in 1770, Thomas in 1772, and Elizabeth who was stillborn in 1777. Nabby, Johnny, Charles, and Thomas lived to adulthood. Abigail Smith Adams improved our world. She lived through and participated in a unique time in American history. By **conferring** with John on all the major government and political issues, as well as voicing her opinions, Abigail set the course for later women. In March of 1776, she wrote to John at the Continental Congress:

> Remember the ladies, and be more generous and favorable to them than your ancestors. Do not put such unlimited power into the hands of the Husbands. Remember all Men would be tyrants if they could. If particular care and attention is not paid to the Ladies we are determined to foment a Rebellion, and will not hold ourselves bound by any Laws in which we have no voice or Representation.

Abigail was only half-joking about women rebelling; both she and John believed women were every bit as capable as men. John joked that women didn't need rights because they already controlled their husbands and their homes!

Abigail was a good farm wife, managing and prospering the farm in John's absence over the years he was tending national business. Her success in this area allowed Abigail to save and invest enough money for the couple to enjoy a comfortable retirement. Abigail was a supporter of women's suffrage. She believed women should be educated and participate in government as men do. Yet it would be more than a hundred years before women would gain the right to vote and the right to be elected to office. Abigail supported the abolition of slavery. The American Revolution convinced her that if Americans should have freedom from a British tyrant, then enslaved people should have freedom from masters. Abigail was impacted by the Boston Massacre, the Battle of Bunker Hill (Abigail was tending the children of Dr. Joseph Warren, who died in that battle), the Battle of Lexington, the occupation of Boston, the first and second Continental Congresses, the Declaration of Independence, the lengthy Revolutionary War, the peace treaty, her husband's work in Europe, the Constitution, her husband's vice presidency and presidency, and the rearing of their children, often alone. The eldest son, John Quincy Adams, later became the sixth American president. Abigail did not live to see this. She died of typhoid fever on October 28, 1818. Abigail was greatly mourned and missed by her husband, children, and other family members and friends.

In 1876 Abigail's grandson, Charles Francis Adams, published Abigail and John's letters to each other in two volumes titled, *Familiar Letters of John Adams and His Wife, Abigail.* These letters are a remarkable window into America's late eighteenth and early nineteenth centuries and the extraordinary life of Abigail Smith Adams!

Activity

    (1) Using the format below, write a letter to a friend.

    (2) Ask someone to proofread your letter to check for spelling and punctuation errors.

    (3) Make a clean copy on stationary or lined paper.

    (4) Mail your letter.

    (5) Anticipate your friend's reply!

Date

Your Street Address
Your Town or City
Your State and Zip Code

Dear_____

(paragraph 1)

_____

_____

_____

_____

_____

(paragraph 2)

_____

_____

_____

_____

(paragraph 3)

_____

_____

_____

_____

_____

Your friend,
(Your Name)

Match vocabulary words with definitions

Use a dictionary to match definitions for the words below, as used in the context of the story.

1. correspondence (noun)
2. establish (verb)
3. garrets (noun)
4. escapade (noun)
5. conferring (verb)

____(a) discussing and consulting something together; comparing ideas and opinions

____(b) attics, usually small cramped ones

____(c) communication by exchanging letters

____(d) to bring into being on a firm or permanent basis; found

____(e) a reckless adventure or wild prank, especially one that is contrary to proper or usual behavior

Answer questions with complete sentences

1. Why should Abigail Adams be remembered?

2. How did Rover accidentally save the gunpowder in the church garret?

3. Why did Abigail and John find a soul mate in each other?

4. Besides reading a biography about Abigail, how could we learn more about her adult life?

Louisa May Alcott: Little Woman with a Big Sense of Duty

LOUISA WAS THE second-born daughter of Abigail May and Bronson Alcott. She entered the world on November 29, 1832. Her father was a teacher who held very **progressive** ideas about education and healthy lifestyles. Bronson believed that girls, as well as boys, deserved a good education. He believed that children should be treated with dignity and respect, just as adults were treated. Bronson valued children's opinions and encouraged his daughters to set goals and to express themselves. Today these ideas are common and would not attract attention. However, such ideas were considered radical and indeed strange by most nineteenth-century standards! Many people still viewed girls and women as being weaker in mind and body than their male counterparts. Education for females was often viewed as a waste of time and money.

Bronson was an inspired teacher. That would seem to be a good trait. However, his methods and ideas were so far ahead of popular opinion that Bronson was fired from nearly every teaching position he acquired. This created an extremely tight budget for the Alcott household that grew to include four daughters as well as the two parents. There was rarely enough money for even necessities. Bronson advocated Grahamism, a diet that was actually very nutritionally sound. It included chicken, fish, plenty of vegetables and fruits, whole grain products, milk, and water. Refined sugar, red meat, and alcohol were avoided. The Alcotts **adhered** to the diet as closely as possible, but they could rarely afford chicken or fish. For this reason, the family's diet was somewhat **deficient** in protein.

In addition to caring for her own family, Abigail took in sewing and laundry from other families to help supplement Bronson's meager income. As diligently as Louisa's parents worked, the family had no financial stability. Louisa and her sisters worked at whatever jobs they could find as soon as they were old enough to help contribute to the family income. Few employment opportunities were available for girls and women. Sewing, cleaning, childcare, and teaching were the bulk of paying positions for females. None of these jobs, including teaching, paid a living wage for women. Male teachers were paid more because it was expected that they would support families. Women were not given this consideration. It was viewed as an embarrassment for women to support their families.

Louisa decided at a young age that she would create financial security for her family. She would find a way to earn enough money to take care of her family's needs. Louisa had always loved to read and write. She kept a journal, wrote and directed little plays to entertain her sisters and cousins, and stole away to the attic every chance she had to read and write in blessed **solitude**. After much thought and careful consideration, Louisa decided writing would be the only avenue she could pursue that could create real income. She was inspired by Harriet Beecher Stowe, the first American woman to actually make a living as a writer. The love and strength of character that Louisa's mother demonstrated greatly influenced her daughter's life. Louisa once wrote, "I think she is a very brave, good woman, and my dream is to have a lovely, quiet home for her, with no debts or troubles to burden her."

Following her unselfish plan, however, would mean personal losses for Louisa. Pursuing a career meant that nearly all hopes of marriage and motherhood would be **sacrificed**. It was rare for women in Louisa's day to have a career and a family. Homemaking was truly a full-time occupation. The basic demands of homemaking required more time and physical energy than they do today. Homemakers had no labor-saving household appliances. They did not have factory-made clothing and a variety of prepared foods and meals available to them. A woman who was a wife and mother was nearly always viewed as being neglectful of her family if she had an outside career. Another problem was that many husbands had trouble dealing with a wife's financial success. A common attitude was that a wife's success somehow made a husband inadequate as the family provider. There was another money dilemma in nineteenth-century America. Most women in Louisa's lifetime lost the legal right to keep ownership of their own money and property once they became married. Legal ownership and control was transferred to their husbands by various state laws of the time. It did not matter if a woman's money and/or property had been inherited or had been personally earned by her. If Louisa had married, her husband might have controlled the income from her books. She might not have been allowed to help her parents, sisters, and other relatives as she wished. This may or may not have been a concern for Louisa. But it was an important consideration for many of her contemporaries.

Louisa's writing inspiration came from life experiences. She wrote about life as she saw it. In September of 1851, at age eighteen, Louisa sold a poem, which she called "Sunlight." The next spring, Louisa sold a short story to a newspaper for $5.00. Over the years she also had experiences as a

Civil War nurse and as a teacher. These endeavors provided Louisa with a rich and varied palette from which she chose to color her stories. *Hospital Sketches*, published in 1863, was a collection of letters Louisa had written to her family while she served as a nurse during the American Civil War. That publication was very successful. For the next few years, she wrote a variety of poems, thrillers, and juvenile tales. In 1867 Louisa worked as an editor of *Merry's Museum*, a children's magazine. Urged by her publisher, Louisa wrote *Little Women* that same year. She was able to write the entire book in two six-week periods. This was because Louisa had most of the story created in her mind by the time she began to put it down on paper. Louisa's own family appeared as the main characters in *Little Women*. The book was so popular that a continuation of its story was published under the same title in May of 1869. With the success of *Little Women*, Louisa earned more than financial security for her family. Her success as a writer actually guaranteed wealth. Louisa had achieved her primary goal of taking care of her family. Never again would money matters trouble the Alcotts.

Little Women was followed by *An Old Fashioned Girl* in March of 1870, *Little Men* in June of 1871, *Eight Cousins* in December of 1874, *Rose in Bloom* in November of 1876, *Under the Lilacs* in April of 1877, *Jack and Jill* in 1880, *Jo's Boys* in 1886, and *A Garland for Girls* in 1888. Louisa's lesser-known writings were *Flower Fables* in 1854, *Moods* in 1864, *Work* in 1870, and *Spinning Wheel Stories* in 1884.

In addition to her mother and father's love, support, and teachings, Louisa was influenced and tutored by two forward-thinking family friends, Ralph Waldo Emerson and Henry David Thoreau. When women gained voting rights on school, taxes, and bond issues in Massachusetts,

Louisa was the first woman to register in Concord. Louisa worked for women's suffrage. She was able to persuade her publisher to print Harriet Hanson Robinson's *Massachusetts in the Woman Suffrage Movement.* The year was 1881. A few years later in 1886, Louisa wrote her last novel, *Jo's Boys.* In it she made good arguments for women's rights and other social reforms. Louisa once wrote, "I can remember when anti-slavery was in just the same state that suffrage is now, and take more pride in the very small help we Alcotts could give than in all the books I ever wrote."

Louisa never married. She never had children of her own. The unselfish author attained her goal of providing financial security for her family by earning enough money to support them her whole adult life. Louisa purchased a special home called Orchard House for her mother, who was affectionately called Marmie. Years before, when it had been financially necessary for the young family to move out of their much-loved family home and into more meager dwellings, Marmie had been very sad. Orchard House was a special gift from daughter to mother. When Louisa's sister Anna died, Louisa became a substitute parent for her niece Lulu and raised the child as her own. Louisa also helped various other needy relatives. She took care of her ailing, elderly father until his death. Bronson died just a few months before Louisa herself died.

Louisa's books have been loved by each generation for a century and a half. Her stories involve universal truths about caring, loving families. *Little Women* was inspired by and modeled after the Alcott family. The character of *Jo*, for all practical purposes, is a very accurate self-portrait of Louisa, herself. In 1888, at the age of fifty-six, gifted author and loving, generous daughter, sister, and aunt, Louisa May Alcott died.

Activity 1

(1) Read the book *Little Women.*

(2) Then watch one of the several movie versions available on video or DVD.

(3) Finally, create a Venn diagram to compare / contrast the book and movie. The Venn diagram is located near the beginning of the book, after the Lesson Options. Check your local video store for availability. There were at least six movie versions of *Little Women* produced during the twentieth century:

1918, starring Dorothy Bernard, Conrad Nagel, and Henry Hull; directed by Harley Knoles

1933, starring Katharine Hepburn, Joan Bennett, and Edna May Oliver; directed by George Cukor

1949, starring June Allyson, Peter Lawford, Margaret O'Brien, and Elizabeth Taylor; directed by Mervyn LeRoy

1970, starring Angela Down and Janina Sayl

1978, starring Meredith Baxter, Susan Dey, and Ann Dusenberry; directed by David Lowell Rich

1994, starring Winona Ryder, Susan Sarandon, Gabriel Bryne, Samantha Mathis, Kirsten Dunst, and Claire Danes; directed by Gillian Armstrong

Activity 2

Louisa found inspiration for many of her stories from her own family.

(1) Each student will write a true short story about an interesting or memorable event that happened in their family.

(2) Students will share stories aloud with family or class.

Activity 3

(1) Have students read any of Louisa's books.

(2) Have students design a book fair poster promoting it.

Teacher or students may decide size of poster board or construction paper to use, as well as decorating mediums such as colored pencils, colored felt-tip pens, crayons, watercolors, etc.

Match vocabulary words with definitions

Use a dictionary to match definitions for the words below, as used in the context of the story.

1. progressive (adjective)

2. adhered (verb)

3. deficient (adjective)

4. solitude (noun)

5. sacrificed (verb)

   ____(a) accepted the loss or destruction of something desirable for a higher cause, end, or ideal

   ____(b) advancing, making continuous improvement toward better conditions, open-minded ideas, and more enlightenment ____(c) seclusion, the state of being alone

____(d) devoted to or followed closely

____(e) inadequate, lacking some element or consideration

Answer questions in complete sentences

1. Why should Louisa May Alcott be remembered?

   _____

   _____

   _____

2. In following the Grahamism diet, what foods were consumed? What food were avoided?

   _____

   _____

   _____

3. What did Louisa sacrifice to become a professional writer?

   _____

   _____

   _____

4. Name at least two reasons why Louisa became a professional writer.

   _____

   _____

   _____

Marian Anderson: "A Voice Like Yours Is Heard Only Once in a Hundred Years"

MARIAN ANDERSON, WHO would become regarded as one of the twentieth century's most talented singers, was also considered one of the best contraltos. That means her voice reached the lowest sound for a woman, between a soprano (highest for a woman) and tenor (midrange for a man). Born on February 27, 1902 in Philadelphia, Pennsylvania, Marian was the eldest of three daughters born to African Americans John and Anna Anderson, a loving, but very impoverished, young married couple. John was a dealer and deliveryman of coal, wood, and ice. Anna had been a schoolteacher before her marriage. The parents raised their young daughters, Marian, Alyce, and Ethel, in the warm environment of family love. Their home was **modest**, yet always cheery and inviting. Music played an important part in the family's life; they enjoyed singing together. As soon as the girls were old enough, they joined in with their parents in singing hymns, spirituals, and old American songs.

Young Marian's musical gift was apparent by the age of three years when she began singing on her own. In addition to playing with Alyce and Ethel, one of Marian's favorite preschool-age games was to sing in a "la-la-ing" fashion. She did this while pounding out an accompaniment on her make-believe piano. Her "piano," in reality, was only a bench!

The **congregation** at Philadelphia's Union Baptist Church enjoyed Marian's first public singing. This was the church she attended with her family. Little Marian sang in the junior choir. By the time she was six years old, she was singing duets with a friend, Viola Johnson. Marian's father purchased a used piano when she was eight. Regrettably, the family could not afford lessons for their **prodigy**. Determined to learn to play the piano, Marian used a little card tucked behind the keys marked with the notes. She plunked away at the keys until she taught herself to play simple accompaniments.

A little later, Marian heard a new sound that intrigued her. This sound had come from a violin. Soon after, a $3.95 violin in a pawnshop window caught Marian's eye. The little girl worked every day after school running errands and scrubbing neighbors' doorsteps for weeks. Marian did this until she earned enough nickels and dimes to buy the violin. A family friend helped her tune the instrument. Before long, string after string broke until the violin was unusable. The fact that Marian had been cheated by the pawn shop dealer did not deter her music quest. By this time, everyone who heard her sing was noticing her full, rich voice. Marian learned and sang all parts in the church choir. She enjoyed the encouragement and love of her family who recognized and appreciated her God-given talent.

When Marian was only ten years old, tragedy struck her family. Her beloved father, John, suffered a head injury and eventually died. Marian, Alyce, Ethel, and their mother, Anna, moved into John's parents' home. The home was large, but full already with an extended family of an aunt, two cousins, and day-care children. Grandmother Anderson was loving and supportive of Marian's singing, but she was also strict. Grandmother was accustomed to giving orders to everyone in the house. Anna became a laundress for other families to help support herself and her young daughters. Sometimes Anna brought the laundry home to wash; other times she worked in her customers' homes. In addition to attending school, Marian went to work cleaning houses to help her mother support their fatherless family.

In high school, Marian decided that learning stenography would enable her to obtain a good-paying job. She had no real interest in such a career choice other than as a means to earn a living wage. What Marian really wanted to do was sing. She could really pour her heart, soul, and talent into this one musical pursuit. Nonetheless, Marian enrolled in a commercial course at William Penn High School for stenographers. The principal recognized Marian's vocal talent when she sang for a school assembly. He recommended that she transfer to South Philadelphia High School to enjoy the fine music program it offered students. Marian acted upon the principal's advice.

As important as music was to her, music was not Marian's only interest. She enjoyed being a Camp Fire Girl. She tried ballet for a short time but abandoned it when she could not afford lessons. Marian also enjoyed spelling bees, large family dinners, speech contests, and church social events.

In time, Marian was a member of the senior choir in her church. The director provided her with every available opportunity to further develop her musical talent. Marian worked diligently, learning all the parts of the anthems. She could substitute for any absent soloist. Marian could even sing an octave higher than required.

Each year the Union Baptist Church held a large concert. Roland Hayes was often the featured performer.

He was the first famous black singer to perform all over Europe. When Marian also performed at the yearly church concert, Hayes took a special interest in her singing. He made valuable suggestions and arranged some opportunities for her to sing in other cities. Until this time, Marian had been a soloist at schools, churches, YWCAs, and YMCAs. Only occasionally had Marian been paid. When she had been paid, the amount was never more than two dollars. Thanks to Hayes's help, Marian gained more experience and became well-known. Marian was soon earning five dollars for each performance. This she was doing while still in high school!

Musicians, in addition to singers, also recognized Marian's extraordinary vocal range and quality. They urged her to take lessons to further channel and direct her abilities. Mary Saunders Patterson, a soprano, gave her free lessons. Soon after, Marian inquired about more advanced lessons at a music school in Philadelphia. While trying to obtain an application for admittance, she was first ignored. When Marian refused to be ignored, she was then hatefully turned away because she was black. This taught her a painful lesson about racial prejudice. Dr. Lucy Wilson, the principal of Philadelphia High School, took Marian to audition for Giuseppe Boghetti. He was a well-respected music teacher who had plenty of students already, but Boghetti was so impressed with Marian's talent that he at once made time for private lessons for her. His fee, however, was too high for Marian to afford. She could not imagine any way to manage the fee. It never occurred to Marian that other people believed in her talent so much that they would not let her dream die! Members of Marian's church began a fundraising drive. The "Fund for Marian

Anderson's Future" began with hoarding pennies and sponsoring benefit concerts. The church raised $500.00 for lessons! When Marian graduated from high school, the Philadelphia Choral Society gave her a scholarship. The National Association of Negro Musicians also provided funds for Marian to continue her lessons.

The same year that Marian graduated from high school, she began traveling and performing at small theaters, schools, and churches. Soon she was not only able to support herself, but her mother as well. Boghetti entered his young student in a contest where Marian won first prize in a competition of three hundred singers. She became the first person to perform with the New York Philharmonic Orchestra. The first time Marian performed there, she lacked the poise that comes with experience. Marian felt inadequate. These weaknesses were evident in her performance. The reviews were not very encouraging. And the fact that Marian was black and the general American public did not always accept people of black heritage worked against her success. Marian's talent was too great to ignore, however. Over the years, as she gained more experience and polished poise, audiences would come to overwhelmingly embrace her performances. This first happened in Europe and then in America.

Marian decided to go to Europe. She studied first in England and then in Germany. Marian met Kosti Vehanen, a Finnish pianist. They toured Scandinavia together, where she was immediately accepted. Marian was invited to the home of the great Finnish composer, Jean Sibelius, and his wife, Aino. Marian was warmly welcomed and complimented. Sibelius commented that he was not sure that the ceilings in their home were high enough for Marian's vocal range!

What a wonderful compliment from someone so renowned in the music world! This meeting was followed by a tour throughout Europe. Arturo Toscanini, a famous orchestra conductor, told Marian, "A voice like yours is heard only once in a hundred years." European concert halls were not large enough to accommodate all the people who wanted to attend Marian's concerts. Sometimes people waited all night in line to purchase tickets. Audiences really related to Marian's music. She included European songs. Marian often sang in the native languages of the countries where she performed. This was no small feat. One of her most favorite songs was *Ave Maria.* First singing it in German, Marian did not fully understand the words until she lived in Germany for a while. She always finished her concerts with a Negro **spiritual** such as "Deep River," "Heaven, Heaven," or "He's Got the Whole World in His Hands." The European audiences found Marian's soulful songs very moving. Marian's fame grew.

On the last day aboard the ship back to America from one of her first European tours, Marian tripped and fell. She broke her foot. The very next evening, December 30, 1935, she was scheduled to perform a concert in New York City's Town Hall. Marian performed beautifully. Without crutches and with her cast hidden under her long, elegant evening gown, Marian leaned gracefully against the curve of a grand piano as she sang. The audience was enthralled with her performance. Marian received a standing ovation!

Over the next thirty years, Marian toured all over the United States and Europe many times. On one occasion, she was scheduled to perform before the Daughters of the American Revolution. The DAR was prevented from allowing this because the landlord of the building used for meetings would not permit an African American person to perform on the premises. This was clearly **prejudice!** One DAR member, First Lady Eleanor Roosevelt, learned of this injustice. She immediately resigned from the organization. Mrs. Roosevelt then arranged for a performance to be held in front of the Lincoln Memorial on Easter Sunday. At first Marian was against this new arrangement because she thought it was too sensational. She did not want to be the center of attention in the incident with the DAR. Marian was raised to be a very modest person and to never let fame sway her. However, there was much support and anticipation from many segments of society for the concert. Marian decided that if it would help the cause of civil rights and freedom for people of black heritage, then her feelings were inconsequential. The free concert "for music lovers and believers in true democracy" was well-received in the spring of 1939. An overwhelmingly large crowd of over seventy-five thousand people attended! They joined Marian in singing the opening song "The Star-Spangled Banner"!

In 1943 Marian married an architect, Orpheus Fisher. He had been her boyfriend during their teenage days. He built a home for his wife and himself in Connecticut. This became Marian's favorite place to relax each summer after completing concert tours. Orpheus called their home and the adjoining property "Marianna Farm" in honor of his wife. When the couple was apart while Marian was out on tour, they stayed in close contact by long telephone calls. Although Marian and Orpheus had no children of their own, they were genuinely fond of children. They enjoyed hosting and entertaining their nephews for weeks at a time.

Marian's career spanned decades. She sang for kings, queens, and three US presidents: Franklin D. Roosevelt, and both Dwight D. Eisenhower and John F. Kennedy at their inaugurations. In 1951 Marian's own government asked her to tour Asia. She was an alternate delegate from the US to the United Nations. In 1955 Marian performed with the New York City's Metropolitan Opera Company. She played the part of Ulrica, a gypsy fortune-teller, in Verdi's *The Masked Ball.* Marian's farewell tour was in 1956 when she toured Europe and the United States. She was very generous with her earnings. She gave to charities, usually anonymously to avoid too much attention to herself. Also in 1956, Marian's autobiography, *My Lord, What a Morning,* was published. It is very straightforward and an interesting read. In 1963 she was awarded the Presidential Medal of Freedom.

Marian succeeded in her career for several main reasons. Thanks to her mother's guidance, she drew strength from her deep faith in God. Marian believed her talent was God-given and that He would guide and direct her in how to use it. From her mother, Marian also learned to stay true to her Christian upbringing. Mother had always told her to practice "grace before greatness." This meant that Marian should strive to remain humble and hardworking. She should not allow success and fame to change her character or strong values. Another reason for Marian's success was that she diligently prepared for every performance. Never taking for granted her talent, Marian practiced her craft so that she might best develop it. In 1993, Marian died at age ninety-one after a long life of sharing her music, which touched the hearts of so many around the world!

Activity 1

Marian has passed from her earthly life, but she lives on in her music.

(1) Purchase a CD of Marian's songs from a music store or borrow one from a library. Her music is also online at Spotify and YouTube.

(2) Discuss just what it was about her voice that caused Arturo Toscanini to say, "A voice like yours is heard only once in a hundred years."

Activity 2

(1) Go on the Internet and research Marian Anderson.

(2) Make a list of some of her songs.

(3) Look over the list and indicate any of the songs that you recognize.

(4) If yes, do you remember when and where you heard the song? Music often connects memories to times and places.

Match vocabulary words with definitions

Use a dictionary to match definitions for the words below, as used in the context of the story.

1. modest (adjective)
2. congregation (noun)
3. prodigy (noun)
4. spiritual (noun)
5. prejudice (noun)

_____(a) an assembly of people brought together for common religious worship

_____(b) a person, especially a child or young person, having extraordinary talent or ability

_____(c) an opinion for or against something or someone without adequate basis

_____(d) free from showy extravagance; simple, small, or plain

_____(e) religious song, especially those originating among African Americans in the southern United States

Answer questions in complete sentences

1. Why should Marian Anderson be remembered?

   _____

   _____

   _____

2. Name two kinds of songs that Marian sang at her concerts.

   _____

   _____

   _____

3. Name two instruments that Marian learned to play as a child.

   _____

   _____

   _____

4. Name some of the people who supported Marian's interest and career in music and explain how they helped her.

_____

_____

_____

Elizabeth Blackwell: First Woman American Doctor

Like so many successful woman of the eighteenth, nineteenth, twentieth, and twenty-first centuries, Elizabeth Blackwell was blessed with forward-thinking parents. They recognized the intellectual abilities of their daughters as well as those of their sons. The Blackwell couple encouraged each of their children to reach their full **potential**.

Elizabeth was born in England in 1827. When she was seven years old, her family moved to America. Her father believed his daughters would have more opportunity to become well-educated in the United States. He worked at various endeavors. He ran a sugar factory. He was also a promoter in the abolition movement to free enslaved people. Abolition was a controversial issue in nineteenth-century America, but Mr. Blackwell chose to act upon his strong personal **convictions**. His beliefs and actions instilled in his children ambition and courage to pursue their heartfelt values and goals. This was a powerful lesson for young Elizabeth. It would serve her well in her long journey in becoming a physician.

Elizabeth's beloved father died when she was seventeen. Grief-stricken, young Elizabeth was angry with the doctors. It seemed to her that they had not known how to help her father. Elizabeth began to think that if she had been a doctor, she might have been able to do something to save her father's life. But in those days, women in America were not doctors. No women had been allowed to attend any American medical school. Therefore, women could not receive the training necessary to become doctors. For a woman to become a doctor seemed ridiculous to nearly everyone, but it did not seem at all ridiculous to Elizabeth! She wanted very strongly to become a doctor but realized her dream would take some time.

Elizabeth began to help her family financially by working as a teacher. This was one of the few occupations open to women. One day, while visiting her mother's sick friend, the woman surprised her by saying, "Elizabeth, you're smart and determined. Why don't you become a doctor?" That was all the encouragement Elizabeth needed!

With the support of her mother, brothers, and sister, Elizabeth began her long journey. She continued to work as a teacher, saving every cent she could. She wrote to medical schools in New York and Philadelphia, but they all refused to admit her. Finally, when Elizabeth was twenty-six, a small medical school in New York offered to admit her. Elizabeth was to find out, however, that her acceptance had been intended as a joke. When a professor read her application to a class of young male doctors-in-training, the students laughed in hilarious glee. They voted overwhelmingly to admit the female applicant. Neither the professor nor his students thought that Elizabeth would actually enroll in the school. Elizabeth was overjoyed when her acceptance notice arrived, believing the college actually wanted her to attend. She could barely wait to begin college!

Elizabeth arrived to her first class full of hope. Immediately, she was teased and laughed at by some students. She was not taken seriously by her professors.

After all, no one really expected her to come or stay when she found that she would indeed be the only female student. But Elizabeth's education and goal to become a doctor was her life's ambition. She plunged head-on into her studies. She asked intelligent questions of the professors. She demonstrated that she was always well prepared for class. Soon, the professors began noticing positive changes in their male students. The once disruptive and rambunctious antics of the young men soon came to be replaced by a calmer, more respectful attentiveness to their professors and their studies. Elizabeth's seriousness of purpose had a calming effect on her male counterparts. They seemed now to be ashamed of their once immature behaviors. Professors commented that with Elizabeth in class, it was much easier to keep order and hold the students' attention during the lectures and discussions. In time, professors and fellow students alike came to respect, admire, and accept Elizabeth as a legitimate student.

After Elizabeth graduated, she traveled to Paris for more advanced training. She had hoped to become a surgeon. But, unfortunately, people in Paris, just like in America, were not open-minded about women being doctors. Elizabeth found a job in a state hospital for poor women. She was not hired as a doctor, however, but as a **midwife** to help deliver babies. It was there that some medicine splashed in one of her eyes. This unfortunate accident caused Elizabeth to lose the sight in her injured eye. Totally blind in one eye, her hopes of becoming a surgeon seemed pointless. Elizabeth went to England, where she treated sick people for a while before becoming terribly homesick. Returning to America, Elizabeth found that women were still not often welcomed as doctors. After saving money for seven years, she opened a little clinic for poor women. It was a struggle because many people still did not accept women as legitimate doctors. But, by working as faithfully as always, Elizabeth's little clinic grew to become a hospital: the New York **Infirmary** for Women and Children.

Her younger sister, Emily, decided to become a doctor also. By 1862, the country was fighting the Civil War. Demand was high for trained nurses to tend the thousands of wounded and ill soldiers. Because Elizabeth knew so much about running a hospital, she was asked to help train nurses. Her professionalism was beginning to be recognized as a valuable asset!

After the war, Elizabeth started a medical school for women. She wanted other women to have an easier time receiving the training they desired. The school was built onto her hospital in 1868. Her sister, Emily, was the able administrator for many years. The hospital later became **affiliated** with Cornell University Medical College after the college was founded in 1898. Elizabeth was one of the founders of the National Health Society of London and the London School of Medicine for Women, where she was professor of gynecology from 1875 to 1907. She wrote *The Physical Education of Girls* in 1852, which was a facts-of-life manual, and *Pioneer Work in Opening the Medical Profession to Women* in 1895.

One of Elizabeth's most important accomplishments in medicine was helping to lower the mortality rate (death rate) of mothers and babies following birth. She did this by establishing a regime of better hygiene. Elizabeth had noticed that mortality rates were higher for women and babies in hospitals than in home birth situations. She rightfully concluded that lack of cleanliness caused infections that quickly spread to other patients.

Elizabeth spent the last years of her life in the quiet village of Hastings, England. She continued to write and lecture. She enjoyed talking to groups of girls and women. When asked what a doctor's goals should be, Elizabeth answered, "To see that human beings are well-born, well-nourished, and well-educated."

Elizabeth died in 1910 at the age of eighty-nine. She had accomplished most of her goals as a doctor and, as a pioneer, had laid the groundwork for future women to prepare for careers in medicine.

Activity 1

One of Elizabeth's contributions to medicine, as well as an improvement in our standard of living, was helping lower the mortality (death) rate for mothers and babies at birth by taking measures to improve hygiene. Although childbirth is usually safe today, in the past, many women and babies died in childbirth or soon after. Most of these deaths were from preventable infections.

(1) Have students compare childbirth death rates for mothers and babies in 1900 with today's rates.

(2) Also, students can compare the average life span for a baby born in 1900 with a baby born today.

Activity 2

(1) Interview a woman doctor and ask:

Why did you become a doctor?

What was your greatest challenge?

What has been your greatest reward?

(2) Write her responses to compare with other students' findings.

(3) Findings will be listed in categories on the board in class.

Match vocabulary words with definitions

Use a dictionary to match definitions for the words below, as used in the context of the story.

1. potential (noun)
2. convictions (noun)
3. midwife (noun)
4. infirmary (noun)
5. affiliated (verb)

____(a) associated closely with

____(b) a woman who assists women in childbirth

____(c) possibility, an ability that may or may not be developed or realized

____(d) a hospital; a place for the care of the sick or injured

____(e) fixed or firm beliefs

Answer questions in complete sentences

1. Why should Elizabeth Blackwell be remembered?

_____

_____

_____

2. Why did it take Elizabeth so long to become a doctor?

_____

_____

_____

3. What prevented Elizabeth from becoming
   a surgeon?

   _____

   _____

   _____

4. What did Elizabeth do to help other women
   become doctors?

   _____

   _____

   _____

Nellie Bly:
First Investigative Reporter

In 1864, Elizabeth Cochrane, who would become known as Nellie Bly professionally, was born in Cochran's Mill, Pennsylvania. As was the case with many women of accomplishment, she was encouraged to read and think. Her family had enjoyed a middle-class lifestyle until her father, a judge, died. The widowed mother and her two daughters lived modestly for a while. Elizabeth's father had left money in trust for his young family. However, the attorney in charge mismanaged it. Elizabeth's adult older brothers were off on their own. She, her mother, and younger sister had little real income. The family's financial situation deteriorated quickly. Elizabeth's mother remarried, but the man was abusive. This probably colored her view that women should have more rights and greatly influenced her future.

Elizabeth felt she must somehow help her family. She was only seventeen years old but felt the need to be resourceful. The usual jobs for women—cleaning, cooking, and teaching—paid very little. They would monopolize most of her day and still not help her family significantly. Elizabeth did not have an extensive formal education, but she was bright, **articulate**, and very well-read. She pored over books and wrote with a passion.

Elizabeth noticed that journalism was one of the few professions that paid women well. One day, she wrote a response to a newspaper editor's article, "What Women are Good For." The editor's position was not really anything different than what was accepted by most people in those days—women were to be wives and mothers and not trouble themselves with men's business outside the home. Elizabeth wrote such a concise, thoughtful **rebuttal** that the editor responded. Not only did he print her letter, but also he asked her to submit more of her ideas.

Elizabeth pinned her hair up on top her head, attempting to look more mature. Confidently, she arrived at the newspaper office. The editor, George Madden, was expecting a middle-aged, matronly looking woman. He just could not believe the rebuttal had been written by a seventeen-year-old! Madden told the teenager that she was too young to be a writer. Elizabeth quickly responded, "If I can do the job, what does age matter?" Madden was impressed and hired her on the spot! The editor had confidence in Elizabeth's ability to do a good job, but he was not sure the reading audience would take her seriously should they learn how young she actually was. After all, George Madden had almost made that mistake himself! Also, Elizabeth's age would have been a source of embarrassment for her family. The public must not learn that the Cochrane family's breadwinner was a female—and a teenage one at that! The family would be further disgraced because the whole community would know that her dead father had failed to provide for the financial security of his family because he had trusted the wrong person. For these reasons, it was agreed Elizabeth should write under a **pen name**. "Nellie Bly," a popular song of the day, came to mind. The determined young woman could earn a decent income to support her family but keep her true identity a secret at the same time. That was how Elizabeth became Nellie Bly professionally!

Nellie became an investigative reporter, often using her small size and youthful appearance to go unnoticed as she got "the scoop" on controversial issues. She went to work in a sweatshop and exposed the deplorable working conditions that exploited young immigrant women in factories. Nellie exposed slumlords for overcharging poor people and letting the apartments deteriorate into filthy, unsafe firetraps. She wrote about divorce and how it placed women and children in poverty. There was much interest in her articles, but also some backlash. This came especially from advertisers whose shameful business practices were exposed and examined in the public forum of newspaper articles. From time to time, the editor assigned Nellie to cover the society beat, reporting about weddings and club meetings and other light "fluff." This was done to calm the advertisers, whose advertising dollars were needed to keep the newspaper profitable. On a six-month work vacation to Mexico, Nellie reported on governmental corruption and poverty for the *Dispatch*. (Later, in 1888, she wrote a book about her Mexican experience, calling it *Six Months in Mexico.*)

In 1887 Nellie left the *Dispatch* newspaper in Pittsburgh and accepted a job offer at *The New York World.* When she left the *Dispatch*, Nellie was earning fifteen dollars a week. This was as much as any top reporter, male or female! *The World's* owner, Mr. Pulitzer, liked her idea for a daring investigation. Nellie wanted to expose the deplorable conditions at Blackwell's Island, the city's insane asylum. Rumors about the filthy, cold, and inhumane conditions were widespread. No one had taken the time and energy to document the plight of the inmates. While the inhabitants should have been called "patients," they were treated as prisoners with no rights. Nellie posed as an insane immigrant girl from Puerto Rico. Once she was inside, she began to act like a normal person. Nobody seemed to notice. Nobody, including several doctors who examined her, even questioned her need to be admitted. After several days, the *Globe* intervened and secured her release. Nellie's insightful, factual articles, "Behind Asylum Bars" and "The Mad House," were wake-up calls to the city to make major improvements. A grand jury investigation ensued. Dramatic changes were made to improve quality of care for patients. (In 1888, Nellie wrote a book, *Ten Days in a Mad House*, about her time in the insane asylum.)

In 1889 Nellie had an idea that would greatly involve the reading audience of the newspaper. She proposed to make an around-the-world trip. This would be an attempt to beat the time of the fictional character, Phileas Fogg, in Jules Verne's book, *Around the World in 80 Days*. This novel was one of the most popular worldwide. Just about everyone had read it! The idea created a great deal of interest. Yet to send a young woman all alone on such a journey seemed out of the question to her editor; he said it was more appropriate to send a man. Nellie threatened to take her idea to a rival newspaper and beat the travel time of any man! Not surprisingly, she received approval to begin the trip. Once again, Nellie's boldness had worked! Contests sprung up. *The World* set up a competition for readers to guess the exact time Nellie would arrive back home. The prize was $250.00—a great deal of money in 1889! The newspaper also developed a parlor board game called *Around the World with Nellie Bly.* Suddenly, everyone was interested in the young, daring twenty-five-year-old and her exciting trip! Nellie set out at 9:30 a.m. on November 14, 1889 from New York City on a ship heading eastward on the Atlantic Ocean. She visited with Jules Verne and his wife in Paris on her travels through Europe. Verne helped her popularity by telling the press that he thought the stakes were stacked against her success. He later admitted he and his wife had never doubted that Nellie would succeed. They had seen firsthand Nellie's determination. Verne thought his pretended doubt would further public interest for Nellie.

Surprisingly, Nellie experienced many of the same **perils** that beset the fictional traveler, Phileas Fogg. One uncanny, nearly identical, mishap included nearly ending up at the bottom of a canyon in a train wreck! Nellie returned home in seventy-two days, six hours, eleven minutes, and fourteen seconds—seven days sooner than Jules Verne's hero! Although Nellie greatly increased the newspaper's circulation, her boss did not offer her a raise. She quit, but Nellie still did well financially while unemployed.

Nellie had become the most popular woman in the world at the time! She made a fortune in lectures and books. She wrote *Around the World in Seventy-Two Days* in 1890. In her day there were no movies or television. The lecture circuit was the way people reached audiences. Suffragettes were encouraged by Nellie's adventure. Nellie was an established figure in journalism. She had become friends with many successful, wealthy people. Pulitzer was able to persuade Nellie back to *The New York World* in 1893. The front page headline proudly declared, "Nellie Bly Again"!

Marriage to someone in Nellie's own age bracket did not seem likely. In 1895, it would have been very difficult for a young man to live in the shadow of such a successful young wife. Not many men could handle that. Nellie met and married Robert L. Seaman, who was seventy-two. He was a millionaire manufacturer from Brooklyn who owned a kitchenware factory. Nellie's success or younger age did not threaten him. They traveled extensively. One of their favorite trips was retracing Nellie's journey around the world. They did it at a much slower, enjoyable pace.

After Robert's death ten years later, Nellie found that her late husband's company was failing. She took over control and proved to be an able manager. For the next ten years, she worked to turn the business around and into a very profitable venture. Introducing the steel barrel for the distilling process, Nellie experienced success as a barrel manufacturer. Nellie not only saved Robert's company, she also founded the Iron Clad Manufacturing Company in 1905. Nellie managed two multimillion-dollar companies for almost a decade. She introduced innovative company policies to greatly improve the working conditions and quality of life for employees. By providing gymnasiums, bowling alleys, and health care, she initiated physical fitness. By providing staffed libraries, Nellie provided opportunities for "mental fitness" as well. She knew that learning to read and write would enable employees to pass tests and earn diplomas. Nellie believed this mental fitness, as well as physical fitness, would greatly improve the overall quality of her employees' lives. She fully appreciated the moral and monetary value in treating her employees with respect and dignity. About the time Nellie decided to retire from business, she found that she had put too much trust in several people. One manager had written fraudulent checks, forging Nellie's signature on them and had stolen much of her company assets. In addition, Nellie's own brother tried to cheat her out of her business interests and personal assets. This was particularly disheartening because Nellie had generously supported him and their mother for many years. Nellie decided to let her attorneys and trusted managers sort it all out. In the meantime, she wanted to put some distance between herself and her troubles. What Nellie did not know was that the outbreak of World War I would change the course of her life!

Just before the onset of World War I, Nellie headed for Europe. At first it seemed that she was in the wrong place at the wrong time, yet her circumstances turned out to be a godsend. Nellie found herself in the middle of one of the biggest stories of the twentieth century. She was even more surprised to find how much she missed her days as a reporter. Nellie contacted her former editor, Arthur Brisbane, who was now with the Hearst newspaper, the *New York Evening Journal*. She remained in Europe for the next four years, covering the conflict as a war correspondent. Nellie stayed mostly in Austria and other localities in Eastern Europe. She saw the war from a different perspective than most Americans. She covered many battleground stories and never seemed to be truly afraid. On one occasion, Nellie was arrested by German soldiers. They had believed she was an English spy! As soon as they learned her true identity, they apologized and allowed her to leave safely. It seemed that everybody knew of the world-famous Nellie Bly!

After Nellie returned to the United States in 1919, she still had legal troubles over the fraud created by her employee and her brother. She lost a fortune. But Nellie did not let the disappointment of betrayal or the reversal of finances dampen her spirits. What she had always enjoyed most was reporting and making a difference in people's lives. Nellie worked for the *New York Evening Journal* for the rest of her life. She was especially proud of her advice column that gave assistance to struggling, destitute women and children. She helped countless widowed and abandoned wives find work that allowed them to provide for themselves and their small children. Nellie also helped many abandoned and orphaned children find loving permanent homes. One little girl, whom Nellie befriended, lived with her the last few weeks of Nellie's life. Soon after, little Dorothy was adopted by a family. Dorothy's new parents would not allow her to talk about her earlier life. Perhaps they did not wish for their daughter to be viewed as a curiosity or celebrity. An author researching Nellie Bly's life interviewed Dorothy when she was an elderly woman. The author learned that Dorothy had enjoyed a full life. She married a loving man and became the mother of two children. Dorothy still remembered the many kindnesses of her **benefactor**, Nellie Bly. There was one aspect of Dorothy's life that she was never able to overcome, however. This was the failure to establish her exact birth date, birthplace, or the identity of her birth parents. Nellie Bly had searched for this information but failed to find it. Even with her husband's extensive efforts, Dorothy was never able to obtain a passport because she lacked her birth documentation. Without a passport, Dorothy could not travel outside the United States. This was something she and her husband had always wished to do.

Nellie was hospitalized for exhaustion several times over the last few years of her life. She refused to slow down her fast-paced lifestyle despite warnings from her doctors that she must get more rest. Nellie seemed driven to help as many women and children as she could in her final time on earth. She simply pushed herself until she collapsed. The last time this happened was just a few weeks after she had brought Dorothy to live with her. Nellie died in 1922 at age fifty-five of pneumonia. This was not a long life by today's standards, but a much fuller life than many people experience. The teenager who took on the responsibility of supporting her family succeeded beautifully. Along the way, Nellie found that she could help improve the lives of countless other people through her investigative reporting and column writing. In addition to her reporting, Nellie proved to be a compassionate employer and manufacturer. She invented investigative reporting and led the way for other investigative reporters to come after her. Nellie showed how to find "the story behind the story"!

Activity 1

The following activity may be assigned as an individual student project or one for a small cooperative group.

(1) Students will plan an around-the-world journey, either retracing Nellie's itinerary or creating their own.

(2) Using today's modes of transportation (minus air travel), have students design a timetable.

(3) Students could search the Internet to follow world news and weather reports for the period of their imaginary trip. Are there any unforeseen natural perils, such as hurricanes or earthquakes, and/or human-made dangers, such as political unrest or wars, that could delay or hinder their travel?

(4) For students in economic classes, creating a budget for their journey would be a practical application of economic principles. Research current rates of exchange for US dollars with the currency of the nations to be "visited."

(5) Students will write reports and present short oral presentations to the class at the conclusion of their "trips."

   a. What did they learn?

   b. In retrospect, was their route wise?

   c. What changes would they make on a second trip?

There is much opportunity for learning, as well as fun, with this activity.

Activity 2

(1) Students will interview someone and ask questions like a newspaper reporter would do.

(2) The interview should include who, what, where, when, and why questions.

(3) Using this information, students will write a newspaper article.

Match vocabulary words with definitions

Use a dictionary to match definitions for the words, as used in the context of the story.

1. articulate (adjective)

2. rebuttal (verb)

3. pen name (noun)

4. perils (noun)

5. benefactor (noun)

_____(a) clear, distinct, and precise

_____(b) the act of providing some evidence or argument that refutes or opposes

_____(c) dangers, risks, jeopardy

_____(d) a person who gives help, especially of a financial nature

_____(e) a name used by a writer other than their own

Answer questions in complete sentences

1. Why should Nellie Bly (Elizabeth Cochrane) be remembered?

   _____

   _____

   _____

2. Why would Nellie Bly's true identity have been an embarrassment for her family when she was a reporter for the *Pittsburgh Dispatch*?

   _____

   _____

   _____

3. What noteworthy undertaking caused Nellie Bly to become world famous?

   _____

   _____

   _____

4. To what causes did Nellie Bly devote much of her time and energies during the last years of her life?

   _____

   _____

   _____

Barbara Bush: Everybody's Mother and Grandmother

BARBARA WAS BORN on June 8, 1925 to Pauline and Marvin Pierce. Her father was president of McCall's Corporation, a company that published a woman's magazine and also clothing patterns. Her great-great-granduncle had been President Franklin Pierce. Her family was very modest about this fact. Barbara grew up in a wealthy family and was educated in private schools. She spent her junior and senior high school years at Ashley Hall in Charleston, South Carolina. She was a serious student who **excelled** in drama.

Barbara met George Bush, her future husband, at a dance during Christmas vacation at home in 1941. George was a senior at Phillips Andover. They began writing to each other. A year and a half later, they became engaged. World War II was well underway. Being patriotic like many young men of that time, George joined the US Navy. At age eighteen, he was the youngest navy fighter pilot. In the fall of 1944, George was shot down over the Pacific off the island of Chichi Jima in the Bonin Islands. His two crewmates died, but George survived. Doug West, a fellow pilot in his squadron, flew over George and pointed him in the direction of the floating life raft. It was later learned that Doug and another pilot fired on an enemy boat that was coming after George. Most certainly, Doug and the other pilot had saved young George's life. For three frantic days, Barbara and her future in-laws knew that George had been shot down but did not know for certain that he had been rescued. Barbara said those stressful days were a blur as she prayed for George to be alive and well. When the navy got word to them that George was safe, Barbara was overwhelmingly thankful and relieved. She continued planning their winter wedding.

Nineteen-year-old Barbara dropped out of Smith College and married twenty-year-old George on January 6, 1945. They had planned a December 17th wedding, but George was unable to obtain his leave for that date. A very practical young Barbara simply crossed out the December date and wrote in the new one on the invitations. January 6th was also the wedding day of George and Martha Washington, who had married almost two hundred years before. What a strange coincidence! The first two presidents named George would share the same wedding date!

After World War II ended, George enrolled in Yale, where he earned a degree in economics in only three years. Barbara and George become parents when George Jr., known to family and friends as George W., was born in 1946. After graduation, the Bushes moved to Texas, where George put his education to work. He built a successful oil business. In time, they had five more children, but their second-born child, Robin, developed leukemia. This was the lowest point of their life. Their beloved daughter had a terminal illness, and there was nothing that either of the young parents could do to stop it. Little Robin died at age three. This was so very **devastating** for the young couple and their young son. George W. remembers how sad his mother had been. One day, she overheard her little boy tell a playmate that he couldn't come out and play. George said he needed to stay inside and play with his mom because she was so sad about his little sister. That was when Barbara realized that she must put her loss behind her and look to her family's future.

George retired from the oil industry after having made enough money to provide for his family. He wanted to spend more time with Barbara and the children and to pursue a career in politics. George had always felt a strong need to serve his country in the arena of politics. Barbara always supported her husband's goals.

George was elected to Congress in 1966. Later, he became the US ambassador to the United Nations during President Nixon's first term. In January of 1973 he became chairman of the Republican National Committee. In 1974 President Ford asked him to assume the role as chief of the US Liaison Office in China. Barbara welcomed this new post. She would be able to spend more time with her husband in China. While he had headed the Republican National Committee, it had been necessary for George to travel extensively. Barbara looked forward to having him "home" with her, even if it was halfway around the world! Their five children chose to stay in the United States, where they were enrolled in boarding schools and colleges. In January of 1976, George became the director of the CIA at the request of President Ford. The couple moved back to the United States. In 1980 George was asked by Ronald Reagan to be his vice presidential running mate. They won the 1980 election and were reelected in 1984. After serving two terms as vice president, George became the forty-first president of the United States.

At each turn in George's political career, Barbara was a supportive partner, enjoying her role as a homemaker, wife, and mother to her large happy family. She thrived in the variety of places and opportunities she encountered along the way. Barbara especially enjoyed their time in China. The Bushes grew to love the people who also came to love them. The little dog that was the Bushes' pet at the time caused quite a bit of interest and confusion. Most Chinese had never seen a dog. This was because dogs had been banished years before in China to rid the country of rabies. Their little dog did not look like any animal the Chinese could identify, causing so much curiosity!

Barbara had already set up housekeeping in thirty homes in forty-four years of marriage by the time they moved into the White House. She had also traveled 1.3 million miles and visited sixty-eight countries before becoming First Lady. Barbara remarked that she felt very lucky to become a First Lady. She thoroughly enjoyed their years as the first couple and has many fond memories of their time in the White House.

Barbara's husband, children, and grandchildren have always been the focus of her life and the source of her greatest joy. There was one time in her life when Barbara felt the need to justify her priorities. She was asked to be a 1990 commencement speaker at Wellesley College in Boston. Some students questioned her **credentials** as a role model for young women. After all, the First Lady had dropped out of college before graduating. Barbara explained what she believes is most important in life.

> For several years, you've had impressed upon you the importance to your career of dedication and hard work. This is true, but as important as your obligations as a doctor, lawyer, or business leader will be, you are a human being first, and those

human connections—with spouses, with children, with friends—are the most important investments you will ever make. At the end of your life, you will never regret not having passed one more test, not winning one more verdict, or not closing one more deal. You will regret time not spent with a husband, a friend, a child, or parent.

The audience's positive reaction was overwhelming! What Barbara had said caused the young women to consider what was truly important in their own lives. Perhaps it would enable them to make more heartfelt decisions and have fewer regrets at the end of their lives.

Mikhail and Raisa Gorbachev were visiting the United States at the time Barbara gave the commencement speech. Raisa accompanied Barbara to Wellesley and to various other places. Raisa observed that people seemed to love Barbara wherever she went. She asked the First Lady about her secret that enabled her to be so universally accepted. Barbara replied that she believed it was "because I threaten no one…I am old, white-headed, and large." The two women discussed many topics, from families to finances. Raisa was surprised to learn that all the Bush children could afford their own homes. In the Soviet Union, homeownership was rare. Housing was scarce and expensive. Even renting an apartment was difficult. Most young people had to wait for years to find even a small modest one. The Gorbachev's own married daughter, along with her husband and child, lived with them. Their daughter was a professional, a medical doctor, yet she and her husband could not afford a home of their own.

Barbara and George are **avid** readers. When Barbara was first lady, her pet project was promoting literacy. In fact, it was an interest she had begun when George was still vice president. Barbara continues even today to work for **literacy**. She feels few things contribute to the well-being and advancement of people as being literate. By the time they left the White House, Barbara had made more than five hundred appearances at literacy events and remains honorary chairperson of the Barbara Bush Foundation for Family Literacy.

Barbara "coauthored" *Millie's Book* with their family pet, Millie. It is a charming book about Millie's experiences as the White House dog. The book was immediately very popular and a huge success. All the profits were lovingly donated to charity. George joked that the dog's biography made more money than his own biography! One of Millie's puppies, Spot, born in the White House, once again became a resident there. Spot was a family pet of President and First Lady, George W. and Laura Bush. Barbara also wrote *C. Fred's Story*, a book about an earlier Bush pet dog. That book earned around $100,000.00. The money was donated to Literacy Volunteers of America and Laubach Literacy Action, two national programs Barbara helped promote. After leaving the White House, Barbara completed her third book, *A Memoir, Barbara Bush*. Published in 1994, it is a very candid, insightful look at one of America's most loved first ladies. Barbara included excerpts from the diary she had kept for three decades.

After the presidency, the Bushes retired to Texas, where their son George W. was elected governor to two terms. During his second term, and with the blessings of his family and fellow state citizens, he ran for and won the presidency of the United States. In 2004 he was overwhelmingly reelected, receiving more votes than any person in our nation's history. Barbara is only the second woman whose husband and son both became American presidents! (Abigail Adams was the first.) Barbara and George's younger son, Jeb, served as the governor of Florida.

In 2004 Barbara's book *Reflections...Life After the White House* was published and appeared in bookstores across the country and beyond. She begins this book with the inauguration of her son George W. and discusses her family's more current history, as well as times long passed. Barbara especially enjoyed sharing memories of her many travels with her husband.

Both Barbara and George place high on the list of "most admired American women and men." Barbara has always answered her own mail. She and George have enjoyed playing tennis, fishing, swimming, and walking together. They say their prayers together each night in bed. Barbara represents what many women view as being successful in today's world. She is a wife, mother, and grandmother of a happy and loving family, whose integrity and strong Christian values shine. Barbara feels she has been blessed with a loving family and a meaningful life!

Activity 1

Barbara's goal has been to promote literacy. To demonstrate just how important literacy is:

(1) Students will keep a log for one day recording every time they use reading skills, being sure to record every instance—even reading nutritional labels on breakfast cereal boxes or directions in a video game.

(2) On the following day, students will share with the class.

(3) Teacher will list reading incidents on the board. It will be surprising to see just how often reading is necessary in our everyday lives.

Activity 2

Barbara believes in mutual respect and kindness among family members. There is an old saying, "It is better to give than to receive." To test this out:

(1) Students will do or say something thoughtful to someone in their family tonight. Besides making the recipient feel happier, students may be surprised at how good they themselves will feel.

(2) Students will share their experiences with the class the following day.

Activity 3

(1) Students will write a paragraph or short essay from their pets' supposed points of view. This can be very

imaginative and fun. Most children have funny stories they enjoy sharing about their beloved pets.

(2) These stories will be read aloud to the class.

Match vocabulary words with definitions

Use a dictionary to match definitions for the words below, as used in the context of the story.

1. excelled (verb)
2. devastating (adjective)
3. credentials (noun)
4. avid (adjective)
5. literacy (noun)

_____(a) evidence of authority, status, rights, or credit

_____(b) enthusiastic, eager, or dedicated

_____(c) ability to read and write competently

_____(d) surpassed or been superior in some respect

_____(e) emotionally overwhelming, greatly troubling

Answer questions in complete sentences

1. Why should Barbara Bush be remembered?

_____

_____

_____

2. What aspects of being a politician's wife has Barbara found especially enjoyable?

_____

_____

_____

3. While First Lady, what did Barbara do to help promote literacy?

_____

_____

_____

4. According to Barbara, at the end of one's life, what might a person regret instead of lost career opportunities?

_____

_____

_____

Marie Curie: "A Good Mother and a Good Scientist"

MARIE CURIE WAS born Marja Sklodowska in Warsaw, Poland, on November 7, 1867. She was the baby in the family of four daughters and one son. Her parents and siblings affectionately called her Manya, which means "baby of the family." Her father taught math and physics at a boys' high school. Her mother conducted a home school where she taught her own children, as well as other people's children, for a fee. Both parents encouraged their children to learn as much as possible. They valued education as a means to a better life.

Life in Poland was difficult. Although the family was very proud of their Polish **heritage**, it was crucial that they be discreet. Russians controlled their government. Russia tried to suppress any Polish patriotism wherever it became evident. The government's goal was to break the will of the Polish people by abolishing their culture and denying good education to their children. The Russians even forbade the Polish language to be taught in the schools. The theory was that an uneducated, broken people, separated from their culture, was easier to control.

Marja showed intellectual gifts at an early age. By the time she was four, young Marja knew her alphabet and was starting to put words together. She had an excellent memory. She was fascinated by all of the glass jars and the microscope in her father's den. When Marja was nearly six, her father's teaching position was cut, and with it, his income was greatly reduced. The family was forced to move into a smaller house and take in boarding children, whom her mother taught. Marja's family lost their own bedrooms and privacy to the boarders. The family slept on makeshift beds in the main living area. The best food at the dinner table was given to the paying boarders. Life was much less carefree for the family. Every summer Marja was sent to visit relatives who lived in the country. She loved the outdoors, the beauty, and the freedom this offered. Her parents felt that this was a therapeutic reprieve from the hardness and seriousness of everyday life in the city.

When Marja was eight, one of the boarders contracted **typhus**. The disease spread to two of her sisters, Bronya and Zosia. Zosia soon died. Big sister Zosia had been almost a second mother and was Marja's closest companion. Not long afterward, Marja's mother died too. She had been ill with tuberculosis for some time. Young Marja was greatly saddened. She missed her sister and mother so terribly.

The child was always an avid reader. Perhaps it helped keep her mind off her grief. Marja began reading everything she could find: textbooks, poetry, novels, and science journals from her father's library. She read in Polish, Russian, French, and German. She learned to shut the rest of the world out when she was reading. As children, her sisters, brother, and the boarders would play tricks on her. One time they rearranged all the furniture around Marja while she sat in a chair in the middle of the room, contentedly reading. Marja failed to notice because she was so intent on what she happened to be reading! The other children found this to be hilarious! (As an adult, she confided in her colleagues that she would not notice if the laboratory blew up under her feet—as long as she was working!)

Even with the presence of the Russians in their community, Marja was surrounded by strong-spirited Polish people. Her history teacher taught the class in Polish. This was forbidden and extremely dangerous. When the Russian officials came on campus, school personnel used a special bell to warn of their arrival and to alert the teachers to be especially careful. Marja's teacher would call on her, a gifted little student, to recite Russian history. Marja would do so in perfect Russian, always deceiving the Russians, who thought they had demoralized the population. Marja continued to excel in her studies. She graduated from high school at age fifteen. She wanted to go to college, but girls were not allowed to attend college in Poland. Marja was emotionally crushed. She said it was as if she was being told to close her mind! Her father sent her to the country relatives, where she at first continued to cry and lose interest in everything.

Marja had time to think and plan while in the country. She decided that since she was not allowed to attend college in Poland, then she would go to where she was permitted—the Sorbonne in Paris, France. Marja would work and save her money until she could afford college. Marja taught children during the day and at night attended the "Floating University." The teachers were Polish patriots who did not want young people to be ignorant. Groups met in secret in different homes to study and discuss history, math, chemistry, biology, and literature. Students were girls who were denied college educations and boys who could not afford college. During this time, Marja also earned money teaching Polish history and literature to working women.

When Marja was eighteen, she and her sister Bronya made plans so that they could earn college degrees. They would both work and save their earnings and take turns supporting each other through college. Bronya went to Sorbonne first while Marja stayed in Poland six more years working and sending money to her sister. Marja worked as a governess.

On November 3, 1891, Marja was finally enrolled in college! She became known as Marie, the French version of her name. She lived in a bare little room, spending a meager amount of money on food. Marie studied every spare minute she was not in class. College was a challenge because the classes were all taught in French. This language was still rather difficult for her. After all, French was not her native language. Her classmates were more advanced in science because they had received better secondary educations. Neither of these obstacles would deter the young woman. They simply made her more determined than ever to work harder. Marie graduated first in her class with an advanced degree in physics just two years later in 1893. One year after that, she graduated second in her class with an advanced degree in math.

Scientists had recently discovered that uranium gave off unexplained rays. We now know that these rays are atomic radiation. Marie wanted to solve this mystery of the 1890s. She met Pierre Curie, a professor of physics at Sorbonne. Their common interest in science developed into a friendship. In time, their friendship grew into romantic love. They were married on July 26, 1895. With Pierre's encouragement and advice, Marie continued research on radioactivity. In 1898 the couple discovered two new **elements**: polonium, which Marie named in honor of her homeland, and radium. For their work they were awarded the Noble Prize for Physics in 1903. This made Marie the first woman to receive the honor. The Curies had two daughters, Irene and Eve. In 1904 Pierre was appointed professor of physics at the University of Paris. A year later, he was named a member of the French Academy.

In 1906 Pierre was struck and killed by a horse-drawn wagon. Once again Marie suffered the loss of a loved one. She focused her energies on raising the couple's young daughters and by burying herself in her research. The university asked Marie to take over her husband's classes. She did this in addition to continuing her research. Marie found a way to make radium pure. This form is still used today to treat cancer patients. Marie was awarded a second Nobel Prize in 1911. This time the award was for chemistry, in recognition of her work on radium and radium compounds. Marie became the first person to win two Nobel Prizes. In 1914 Marie became the head of the Paris Institute of Radium. She also helped found the Curie Institute.

Even with the worldwide recognition that came with the honors, Marie remained a modest person. She was one of the most famous women in the world at the time, yet she never let her fame make her arrogant or self-centered. Quite the contrary, Marie used her research and award money to help people. Her **generosity** helped set up portable X-ray units in World War I European field hospitals. The injuries of wounded soldiers were quickly assessed and treated. This alone helped save the lives of many young men. By that time, Marie's daughter Irene was also a research doctor and had joined her mother in her work.

Marie grew weaker in her final years. She died on July 4, 1934 in Haute-Savoie from pernicious anemia. Doctors came to realize that the ailment was a form of radiation poisoning that caused leukemia from Marie's many years of radiation overexposure in the lab. To this day, Marie's lab notes are radioactive and will remain so for a long, long time.

Money and glory were not important to Marie Curie, even though she had earned worldwide fame. Marie wanted to be remembered simply as "a good mother and a good scientist." She appreciated the opportunities her education had given her. She had **dedicated** her adult life to finding ways science could improve the lives of humankind. Although Marie endured hardships and personal losses early in her life, she was a selfless scientist who used her God-given talents and abilities so that life might be easier for others.

Activity 1

Have each student write a paragraph explaining how X-rays have been helpful in his/her life. Has illness or injury necessitated an X-ray? Has a family member or pet been x-rayed?

Activity 2

Have each student draw a picture of himself, herself, a family member, or pet behind an X-ray screen showing an X-ray of the body part being examined.

Match vocabulary words with definitions

Use a dictionary to match definitions for the words below, as used in the context of the story.

1. heritage (noun)
2. typhus (noun)
3. elements (noun)
4. generosity (noun)
5. dedicated (verb)

_____(a) unselfishness, willingness and eagerness to share with others

_____(b) traditions handed down from one's ancestors

_____(c) basic substances that cannot be separated into simpler substances

_____(d) a serious and potentially fatal disease characterized by reddish spots on the skin, severe headache, sustained high fever, and extreme weakness or exhaustion

_____(e) wholly committed or devoted to something such as a cause, goal, or purpose

Answer questions in complete sentences

1. Why should Marie Curie be remembered?

   _____

   _____

   _____

2. What evidence showed that Marie was intellectually gifted at a young age?

   _____

   _____

   _____

3. What obstacles did Marie face and overcome in achieving a college education?

   _____

   _____

   _____

4. What evidence shows that Marie remained hardworking and modest throughout her entire professional life?

   _____

   _____

   _____

Jan Davis: NASA Astronaut

NANCY JAN DAVIS was born on November 1, 1953 in Cocoa Beach, Florida, but she considers Huntsville, Alabama to be her hometown. Jan has one brother, who is nine years younger. Her mother was a schoolteacher, and her father was a psychologist while she was growing up. Achievement was an encouraged family trait. Half her heritage comes from her German ancestors, who endured the hardships of settling in Texas during the 1850s. On the other side of the family, pioneer ancestors were English and French immigrants who worked hard to build new lives in a new country.

As a child, Jan liked to read **biographies** and *Nancy Drew* mysteries. It is not surprising that she would grow up to have adventures of her own! Jan graduated from Huntsville High School in 1971. She received her bachelor of science degree in applied biology from Georgia Institute of Technology in 1975. Two years later in 1977, the future astronaut earned a bachelor of science degree in **mechanical engineering** from Auburn University in Auburn, Alabama. Soon after, she joined Texaco in Bellaire, Texas, working as a petroleum engineer in tertiary oil recovery. That is the oil obtained in the third stage of drilling where between 30–60% of the oil in the original reservoir can still be obtained.

While growing up, Jan never considered becoming an **astronaut**. This was because all the astronauts had been male test pilots. It was not a field open to women. The young scientist did not think about a career as an astronaut until NASA selected the first female trainees in 1978. That was when the idea of a career in space began to interest Jan as a very real possibility.

In 1979 Jan went to work for NASA, beginning at Marshall Center as lead engineer of the team responsible for the structural analysis and verification of the Hubble Space Telescope, the telescope servicing mission, and the Chandra X-ray Observatory. Jan was also the lead engineer on the redesigning of the Space Shuttle Solid Rocket Booster External Tank attach ring. She began graduate school. Jan enrolled in flight training and became a pilot, setting her goal to become an astronaut! In 1983 Jan earned a master of science degree in mechanical engineering. She earned her doctorate in 1985 from the University of Alabama at Huntsville.

In 1987 Jan began her training in Houston as soon as she was selected to be an astronaut. This preparation was very intense. It included learning about the space shuttle systems with classroom instruction, workbooks, and **simulators**. Jan needed to learn all she could about geography, meteorology, geology, oceanography, astronomy, materials science, medicine, and anything else that seemed useful to the complex demands placed on a NASA astronaut. Jan's already extensive college degrees gave her a valuable foundation on which to build. She trained as a missions specialist and learned extravehicular activity (space walks) and operation of remote manipulator systems (robot arms) as well as photography, computers, and speech making. Jan remarked that her training and work is very interesting but requires a great amount of time.

Jan's first journey into space was aboard the space shuttle *Endeavor* in September 1992. She performed some of the forty-three scientific experiments in the joint venture with Japan. Her second space flight was on the *Discovery* in February 1994. Her main job was to operate the robotic arm.

Jan's third mission was on the *Discovery* in August 1997. As the **payload commander**, she was responsible for coordinating all the experiments on the space shuttle. On that same mission, Jan operated two robotic arms: the space shuttle arm and a new Japanese robotic arm for the International Space Station. The robotic manipulator arms are essential for docking payloads and cargo to the space station. One of the goals of the space station is to manufacture products and conduct biological experiments in microgravity.

Jan said the achievement of which she is most proud is flying the space shuttle. She loves the view through the window of the earth two hundred miles below. Jan remarked that it is "a very beautiful and awesome sight!" She also thinks that floating in space is really a lot of fun and makes it "very easy to work and move around." While in space, Jan's day consisted of twelve hours of work; two hours before and after each shift to eat, bathe, dress, and do chores; and eight hours to sleep securely strapped into a sleeping bag-type bed. All this is accomplished in zero gravity, making the activities a bit challenging, but fun, nonetheless!

Jan oversaw development of the International Space Station's connecting nodes 2 and 3, multipurpose logistics modules, commercial express racks, and environmental and life-support systems. She also supervised the Payload Operations Center, the science command post at Marshall Center that links earth-bound researchers worldwide with the space station. Her team worked very closely with the

Boeing Company that built and tested structural elements and truss segments of the space station.

Jan has received many honors including: NASA's Outstanding Leadership Medal, Exceptional Service Medal, three Space Shuttle Flight Medals, Marshall Space Flight Center Director's Commendation, Alpha Xi Delta Woman of Distinction Award, Distinguished Engineering Alumni Academy at the University of Alabama at Huntsville, and is an American Society of Mechanical Engineers Fellow, which is the highest honor the society bestows.

Jan has authored several technical papers, holds a patent, and is still a registered engineer.

In addition to her career, Jan has volunteered with the Girl Scouts and been a member of the Lakeview Quilters Guild. Jan also enjoys airplane flying, ice-skating, snow skiing, water sports, and needlepoint. When asked if she has any advice for young people, Jan responded, "Select a field that you will enjoy studying, do your best, and if you do not achieve your goal the first time, keep trying."

Activity

Have students think about their life goals. What would they really like to achieve? Has anyone ever told them that their ideas were foolish or silly? Nearly everyone was told that at one time or another. Think about Elizabeth Blackwell or Nellie Bly. Instill in them the can-do attitude of winners!

(1) Students will think about their life goals. (What would they really like to accomplish as adults?)

(2) Students will take inventory of their skills and interests.

(3) Students will develop a plan to achieve their goals.

(4) Students will write a paragraph or more.

(5) Students will share paragraphs aloud in class.

(6) Students will pay each other sincere compliments such as, "I think you would make a great firefighter because you stay calm in emergencies" or "I think you could be a competent author because you come up with great stories."

Match vocabulary words with definitions

Use a dictionary to match definitions for the words below, as used in the context of the story.

1. biographies (noun)

2. mechanical engineering (noun)

3. astronaut (noun)

4. simulators (noun)

5. payload commander (noun)

_____(a) highly trained pilot who holds multiple degrees in various sciences and travels into outer space

_____(b) a branch of engineering making practical use of pure sciences dealing with the design and production of machinery

_____(c) laboratory devices used for the purpose of training or experimentation that enable the operator to reproduce under test conditions phenomena likely to occur in actual performance

_____(d) the person in charge of the cargo transported on a space shuttle such as satellites or medical or scientific experiments

_____(e) written histories of persons' lives

Answer questions in complete sentences

1. Why should Jan Davis be remembered?

   _____

   _____

   _____

2. What kinds of books did Jan like to read when she was a child?

   _____

   _____

   _____

3. Why did Jan not consider a career as an astronaut earlier in life?

_____

_____

_____

4. What advice did Jan offer about achieving your goals?

_____

_____

_____

Amelia Earhart: Record-Setting Aviator

AMELIA EARHART WAS born on July 24, 1897 in Atchison, Kansas, to Edwin and Amy Earhart. As is true of many high-achieving women, Amelia's parents were open-minded and forward-thinking. They encouraged their daughters to pursue their own interests and not allow gender to deter them. Lovingly, they called her Meelie. Her sister, Muriel, was nicknamed Pidge when she joined the family two years later. Meelie and Pidge grew up in the Midwest, often traveling with their parents. Edwin was an attorney for the railroad. His work often took him out of town. The young parents thought these traveling opportunities were educational for their daughters.

Sometimes, when their parents were on the road during the school year, Meelie and Pidge stayed at the home of their grandfather and grandmother Otis. The grandparents were much stricter than the parents were. The girls, however, were much loved and surrounded by cousins and friends; life was fun and adventuresome. Much to Grandmother Otis' dismay, Amelia was a tomboy! She was not content to play quietly like the little lady she was expected to be. One time, Meelie, Pidge, and their cousins used some boards to build a roller coaster that extended down from the hen house. Amelia was the test pilot for that contraption and crashed at the bottom but was unhurt and undeterred!

Another time Amelia asked for a basketball and a little rifle for Christmas, which of course her parents gave her. She became such a good shot that she kept down the rat population in the barn. Amelia begged for a boy's sled, the kind that was to be ridden lying on one's stomach. This probably saved Amelia's life. Once when she was sliding down a hill, a horse-drawn wagon pulled into her path. She slid safely between the horse's legs under his belly. If Amelia had been on a girl's sled, she would have been sitting upright and crashed headlong into the side of the horse, no doubt dying or at least being gravely injured from the impact.

Amelia's future was **foreshadowed** at the 1908 Iowa State Fair when at age eleven she saw her first airplane. But it was years later before she enjoyed her first flight aloft. Amelia was a serious student all through elementary and high school. Her interests were many. She enjoyed sports, but most sports were not open to girls. Most people thought active sports were unhealthy for girls' bodies, which were viewed as much weaker than those of boys. Amelia always felt she could have excelled if more active sports training had been made available for girls.

Amelia began college at Columbia University. She found many majors interesting yet did not find one that held her interest long. Something seemed to be missing. Amelia felt she should be pursuing something but could not identify just what it was. In 1918, after seeing scores of wounded soldiers returning from World War I, Amelia dropped out of college and became a nurse in Toronto, Canada. For a while she seriously considered a career as a doctor, but after her first airplane ride, she was absolutely hooked on flying! Amelia worked as a telephone operator to afford flying lessons and to save money for the purchase of her very own airplane.

In 1921 Amelia bought her first airplane, a Kinner Airster. Soon she began entering flying contests and setting records. This was an unusual activity for women in those days. Flying was a very dangerous pursuit. There were few safeguards or equipment for navigation. In the early 1920s, navigation usually meant looking out the window to see the landscape below. There were some instruments, but very primitive compared with modern equipment. As a means of transportation, airplanes were in their infancy.

In 1927 Amelia was offered a chance to become the first woman to cross the Atlantic by airplane. Ruth Nichols sponsored the flight and wanted to complete it herself, but family obligations prevented her from doing so. Her family was afraid she would be killed! Much of the flight was in fog. Because Amelia had no training on instrument flying, she did not actually pilot the plane and, as she said, went along like "a bag of potatoes." Even though she had not piloted the airplane, it was so unusual for a woman to be included on such an adventure. A great deal of attention was focused on Amelia. She promised herself that on the next Atlantic crossing, she would solo—that is, she would fly alone. Amelia wrote her first book *20 Hours, 40 Minutes* describing her first Atlantic crossing.

In the early part of the twentieth century, air travel was much more hazardous with few instruments to aid pilots. When Amelia **soloed** the Atlantic on May 20–21, 1932, she arrived off the coast of Ireland over two hundred miles from Paris, France, her intended destination. It was not unusual to be many miles off course. Amelia's trip was the fifth anniversary of Charles Lindbergh's historic flight.

She became an instant celebrity! Amelia was celebrated in Europe and America. President Herbert Hoover presented the National Geographic Society's Gold Medal to her. New York City honored the heroine with a tickertape parade on Broadway.

Amelia's escapades drew attention nationally and beyond. She piloted an autogiro, an early helicopter-type aircraft. She set a woman's record for nonstop transcontinental flight—Los Angeles, California to Newark, New Jersey, in nineteen hours, five minutes. In 1935 she became the first person to solo the Pacific Ocean from Honolulu, Hawaii, to Oakland, California. When asked why she had flown from Hawaii to California instead of the other direction, Amelia answered, "It is easier to find a continent than an island." This simple truth would prove painfully accurate on her round-the-world trip two years later. In April of 1935, AE (what she preferred to be called) soloed from Los Angeles to Mexico City in seventeen hours, seven minutes. Then she soloed from Mexico City to Newark, New Jersey, where welcoming crowds surrounded her airplane. With her popularity and her husband's promotional efforts (she had married George Putnam in 1931), AE secured a twin-engine Lockheed Electra airplane financed by Purdue University and dubbed the Flying Laboratory. Amelia began to plan her round-the-world flight, which was to be her last big hurrah before retiring from stunt flying and then writing a book about her global adventure. The trip started from Oakland, with a landing in Hawaii in March of 1937. Departing Hawaii, the plane had a flat tire and crashed on takeoff, causing damages that necessitated shipping the plane back to California for repairs.

When the airplane was finally ready several months later, the direction of the trip was changed to avoid the

monsoons in the Pacific and Indian Oceans. Instead, Amelia and her navigator, Fred Noonan, would fly from west to east. The journey started out well. They took off from Miami, Florida, on June 1, 1937, crossing the Caribbean, the coast of Brazil, across the Atlantic, over Africa, India, Southeast Asia, Indonesia, Australia, and to New Guinea. On July 2, they left Lae, New Guinea, and headed for Howland Island, a tiny one-mile by two-mile spot in the Pacific. From there they would make the last stop, Hawaii, and then move on to California. Amelia's aircraft never reached Howland Island. The US Navy's *Itasca* was on standby near Howland Island. Although there was brief radio communication with the airplane, the navy could never locate Amelia's plane's position. The navy sent out messages in Morse code, not realizing that neither Amelia nor Fred had learned how to decode it. Had the fliers been able to do so, they might have been located and rescued. The US Navy launched the most extensive sea and air search ever but could not locate the airplane or the fliers.

The disappearance of Amelia Earhart and Fred Noonan has remained a mystery for nearly eight decades. Over the years theories have come and gone. One of the wildest was that AE and Fred were spies gathering **reconnaissance** of Japanese-held islands for the American military just before the impending outbreak of World War II. There has never been any solid evidence to support this claim, however. Another scenario was that the fliers landed on a Japanese-held island and were imprisoned or killed as prisoners-of-war. There have been several accounts of witnesses remembering people who vaguely fit the fliers' descriptions, but no real proof has surfaced. The most likely scenario seems to be that AE was off course—as she so often had been before—and the plane simply ran out of fuel and crashed in the vast Pacific Ocean.

AE had sent notes home, to her husband, whom she affectionately called GP, at each stop on the journey, detailing each leg of the trip. GP compiled her notes and published them as a book, calling it *Last Flight*.

As with every person, Amelia had weaknesses as well as strengths. Her strengths were her determination and courage to pursue her dreams. Her weaknesses were refusing to include every safety precaution available to be as prepared as she could have been. Amelia declined to take along the tracking equipment. She wanted to make as much room as possible for cans of fuel. Amelia never bothered to learn Morse code and to really learn all she could about her increasingly complicated aircraft. Had she done so, the outcome may have been very different for this **aviator**. Instead, her weaknesses cost her own life, as well as that of her navigator. Because of Amelia's demise, safety precautions were put into practice. Perhaps Amelia's philosophy of life and perhaps an eerie foreshadowing of her death were clearly stated on January 8, 1935 when she said:

> Please know that I am quite aware of the hazards. I want to do it because I want to do it. Women must try to do things as men have tried. When they fail, their failure must be but a challenge to others.

Activity 1

Have students choose a place that AE landed on her round-the-world trip and write a short description, including:

(1) city and country, including its absolute location (latitude and longitude),

(2) average temperature for June–July,

(3) 1937 and current population,

(4) official language,

(5) terrain and landforms.

These brief reports will be shared with the class.

Activity 2

Make models of any of AE's airplanes, an autogiro, or a boy's sled and a girl's sled that were popular during her childhood.

Activity 3

The teacher can create a scavenger hunt by giving class absolute locations (latitudes and longitudes of specific places) and having students identify each of those places AE landed over the course of her flying career.

Activity 4

Using the transcript of the radio transmissions between the navy ship *Itasca* and Amelia's airplane, create a readers' theater for class presentation. The transcript can be located at the end of Amelia's book *Last Flight*.

Match vocabulary words with definitions

Use a dictionary to match definitions for the words below, as used in the context of the story.

1. foreshadowed (verb)

2. soloed (verb)

3. monsoons (noun)

4. reconnaissance (noun)

5. aviator (noun)

____(a) flew an airplane alone without a companion or partner

____(b) showed or indicated beforehand

____(c) a pilot of an airplane or other heavier-than-air aircraft

____(d) seasonal winds in the Indian and Pacific Oceans that usually bring heavy rains to southern and western areas of Asia

____(e) exploratory military survey of enemy territory

Answer questions in complete sentences

1. Why should Amelia Earhart be remembered?

_____

_____

_____

2. How was Amelia's childhood different from that of most other girls during the early years of the twentieth century?

   _____

   _____

   _____

3. If Amelia had survived her round-the-world flight, what do you think she would have done with the rest of her life? Why?

   _____

   _____

   _____

4. If Amelia had lived in our time, what do you think she would be doing today? Why?

   _____

   _____

   _____

Ruth Heller: Author and Illustrator of Children's Books

RUTH HELLER WAS born on April 2, 1923 in Winnipeg, Manitoba, Canada. Her father was very concerned about the kind of environment that his family would make their permanent home. When Ruth was just one year old, her parents and brother, Daniel, moved to Vancouver in British Columbia to await **immigration** to the US. Her father had traveled extensively, looking for the best place to settle the family. He decided that San Francisco, California, was the **ideal** city.

Ruth was ten years old before her family was allowed to make San Francisco their permanent home. Looking back over her life, Ruth noticed that many of the scenes of her childhood were evident in her artwork. In Vancouver, many of the streets in her neighborhood had been named after queens and kings. Some of her stories included fancy-clothed royalty. The beautiful Canadian beaches **inspired** her fish, shells, and sea creatures that decorated some of her books. Her butterfly pictures came from her memories of a huge willow tree where she had collected caterpillars caring for them until they became gorgeous butterflies.

Growing up, Ruth enjoyed coloring, drawing, and reading. It was not surprising that she would choose to study art when she was ready for college. Ruth graduated with a fine arts degree from the Berkeley campus of the

University of California, where she studied painting and art history.

Ruth married Henry Heller and had two sons. After the boys were in elementary school, Ruth returned to college for an additional two years, studying art design and drawing at the California College of Arts and Crafts. Designing gift-wrap, other paper products, and newspaper ads were her first jobs. As a **freelance** designer, Ruth created posters, puzzles, and coloring books.

Ruth's first book, *Chickens Aren't the Only Ones*, started as an idea in 1970, but she could not find anyone to publish it for ten years. In May 1980 Ruth spent a whole month at a special place in Saratoga, New York, where artists and writers worked to fine-tune their projects. Her new, improved book was published in 1981. Ruth continued writing and illustrating for several decades. Many of her books are as educational as they are **aesthetically** pleasing. Ruth once explained her work:

> All my books are nonfiction picture books in rhyme. I find writing enjoyable and challenging, and I think it is an easy way for children to learn new facts and acquire a sophisticated vocabulary. Children are not intimidated by big words. I try to make my writing succinct and allow the illustrations to convey as much information as possible.

Ruth remained with her family in San Francisco for the rest of her life, truly enjoying her family life and work life. Ruth passed on in 2004 after a struggle with cancer. She wrote and illustrated many books and illustrated a few books for other authors. In each you will be amazed at the glorious, colorful details that make her books so popular for pure pleasure as well as educating children. The following are a long list of Ruth's books sorted by categories:

Coloring books

* *Color and Puzzle* (1968)

* *The Oriental Rug Coloring Book* (1973)

* *Designs for Coloring* (1976)

* *Designs for Coloring: More Designs* (1976)

* *Designs for Coloring: 3* (1977)

* *Designs for Coloring: 4* (1977)

* *Designs for Coloring: Jumbo* (1980)

* *Creative Coloring Activity: Designs by Ruth Heller* (1981)

* *Designs for Coloring: Stitch* (1984)

* *Designs for Coloring: Owls* (1985)

* *Designs for Coloring: Geometrics* (1990)

* *Designs for Coloring: Butterflies* (1990)

* *Designs for Coloring: Cats* (1990)

* *Designs for Coloring: Birds* (1990)

* *Designs for Coloring: Flowers* (1990)

* *Designs for Coloring: Snowflakes* (1990)

* *Designs for Coloring: The Hebrew Alphabet* (1991)

* *Designs for Coloring: Optical Art* (1992)

* *Designs for Coloring: Seashells* (1992)

* *Designs for Coloring: Tropical Fish* (1997)

* *Designs for Coloring: The Far East* (1997)

* *Designs for Coloring: Ancient Egypt* (1999)
* *Designs for Coloring: More Flowers* (1999)
* *Designs for Coloring: Prisms* (2000)
* *Designs for Coloring: Insects and Spiders* (2000)
* *Stained Glass Designs for Coloring: Geometrics* (1998)
* *Stained Glass Designs for Coloring: Snowflakes* (1998)
* *Stained Glass Designs for Coloring: More Geometrics* (2000)

Children's books

* *Chickens Aren't the Only Ones* (1981)
* *Animals Born Alive and Well* (1982)
* *The Reason for a Flower* (1983)
* *Plants That Never Ever Bloom* (1984)
* *How to Hide a Butterfly and Other Insects* (1992)
* *How to Hide an Octopus and Other Sea Creatures* (1992)
* *How to Hide a Polar Bear and Other Mammals* (1994)
* *How to Hide a Crocodile and Other Reptiles* (1994)
* *How to Hide a Meadow Frog and Other Amphibians* (1995)
* *How to Hide a Parakeet and Other Birds* (1995)

Language books

* *A Cache of Jewels and Other Collective Nouns* (1987)
* *Kites Sail High: A Book About Verbs* (1988)
* *Many Luscious Lollipops: A Book About Adjectives* (1989)

* *Merry-Go-Round: A Book About Nouns* (1990)
* *Up, Up, and Away: A Book About Adverbs* (1991)
* *Behind the Mask: A Book About Prepositions* (1995)
* *Mine, All Mine: A Book About Prepositions* (1997)
* *Fantastic! Wow! And Unreal! A Book About Interjections and Conjunctions* (1998)
* *Color* (1999)
* *A Sea Within a Sea: Secrets of the Sargasso* (2000)
* *Galapagos Means Tortoises* (2003)

Illustrations

* *The Egyptian Cinderella* by Shirley Climo (1991)
* *Kings of the Birds* by Shirley Climo (1991)
* *King Solomon and the Bee* by Dalia Hardof Renberg (1994)
* *The Korean Cinderella* by Shirley Climo (1996)
* *Blue Potatoes, Orange Tomatoes* by Rosalind Creasy (2000)
* *Merriam-Webster's Primary Dictionary* (2005); published posthumously
* *Merriam-Webster's Alphabet Book* (2005); published posthumously

Activity

One of the art techniques employed by Ruth is trace drawing.

(1) Create a trace drawing by tracing a picture or design onto smooth watercolor paper with strong pencil lines.

(2) Then turn your traced picture facedown onto another piece of paper and rub on the lines with a Popsicle stick to transfer the drawing.

(3) Next, trace carefully over the pencil lines with a fine-tipped black felt pen.

(4) Color in your picture with colored pencils, markers, or crayons.

Match vocabulary words with definitions

Use a dictionary to match definitions for the words below, as used in the context of the story.

1. immigration (noun)
2. ideal (adjective)
3. freelance (adjective)
4. aesthetically (adverb)
5. inspired (verb)

    ____(a) influenced, moved, or guided emotionally or intellectually

    ____(b) beautifully appealing to the mind and emotions

____(c) independent, working, or pursuing a profession without a long-term contract or commitment to any employer

____(d) regarded as perfect in its category, excellent, or highly desirable

____(e) movement into a country of which one is not a native and taking up permanent residence

Answer questions in complete sentences

1. Why should Ruth Heller be remembered?

_____

_____

_____

2. Why did Ruth live in several different communities as a child?

_____

_____

_____

3. What were Ruth's first paid jobs as a professional artist?

_____

_____

_____

4. How is Ruth's childhood reflected in her artwork?

_____

_____

_____

Mahalia Jackson: Queen of Gospel

MAHALIA JACKSON WAS born in 1911 in the slums of New Orleans. She lived with her African American parents and five brothers and sisters in a three-room shack. Her father loaded cotton bales onto the boats docked at the Mississippi River on weekdays. On weekday evenings and on Saturdays, he worked as a barber. On Sundays he preached at the Holiness Church. Mahalia's mother cleaned house for a wealthy white family. Even with all the hard work of the parents, the family was extremely poor. There was no money for any extras, such as toys or even a Christmas tree. As a child, Mahalia never owned a doll.

When she was only five years old, Little Haley lost her mother. The poor woman had literally worked herself to death. Haley and ten-year-old brother Peter went to live with Aunt Duke and Uncle Emmanuel. Aunt Duke worked as a servant and cook for a wealthy white family, and most of Haley's "new" dresses were **castoffs** or hand-me-downs from the daughters of that wealthy family. The neighborhood children sometimes made fun of Haley for wearing discarded clothes. Haley and Peter loved visiting their father at the barbershop on Saturdays. These visits were the high point of each week for the children and their father.

Haley worked even as a child. On weekday mornings she helped dress the children of a wealthy family before she could go to school herself. Haley often arose at sunrise to help Uncle Emmanuel weed the vegetable garden and feed the chickens, pigeons, and goats. Peter did yard work for a wealthy family. The children and their uncle often caught shrimp, crabs, and even small alligators from the river for their dinner. These activities were essential for survival. Without the garden, animals, and river catches, the family would not have had enough food.

Haley loved to sing even when she was playing with her siblings, cousins, and friends in the neighborhood. When Haley was still only five years old, the minister of her church asked her to join the choir. This was her singing **debut**. Later as an adult, Mahalia remarked, "I had a big voice even then!" Growing up in New Orleans provided her with a rich exposure to music. There were dockworkers who sang to ease their drudgery, lively church hymns, brass bands on street corners, and phonograph records of blues songs. Of all the blues singers, Bessie Smith was young Mahalia's favorite. She especially loved Bessie's version of *St. Louis Blues*.

Chicago was the place that Mahalia most wanted to see. She had heard wonderful stories about how blacks were treated with more respect in the North than she had experienced in the South. She continued to work and save her money by doing laundry for white people. By the eighth grade, Mahalia quit school to work full-time babysitting and doing laundry.

In 1927 at age sixteen, Mahalia went to Chicago with her visiting aunt Hannah, who offered to let her come live with her and enroll in nursing school. These plans to become a nurse never came to be realized. Aunt Hannah developed heart problems, making it necessary for Mahalia to go to work at once to help pay their living expenses. In her spare time Mahalia began to volunteer at the Greater Salem Baptist Church, where she auditioned and joined the chorus. The church members loved her rich, deep voice. When the minister's sons formed the Johnson Gospel Singers, Mahalia was asked to join them. The group became the most popular singing group in black churches in Chicago. News of their singing spread quickly, and soon Mahalia was invited to sing in many black churches, some as far away as St. Louis, Missouri.

By that time, Mahalia was earning money doing what she loved to do most. This was during the 1930s when the Great Depression had put many people out of work. Her singing not only enabled her to earn a living, but introduced black **gospel music** to a worldwide, multiracial audience.

Mahalia's popularity led to tours. In addition to live performances, she made records, which became very popular across the whole country. Her first record was *God's Gonna Separate the Wheat From the Tares* on the Decca label. In 1946 she recorded *Moving On Up a Little Higher* on the Apollo label. Many famous black entertainers invited her to sing with their bands. Mahalia declined their offers, saying, "I have no desire to sing the blues. They are too sad. I prefer to sing songs of hope and faith."

Mahalia made her debut at Carnegie Hall in New York City in 1950. This was an important milestone in her career. Mahalia's singing won the hearts of many people, both blacks and whites. She sang for the empress of Japan. She sang in the White House for President Eisenhower on his birthday. She also sang for President Kennedy the night before his inauguration.

During the days of the Civil Rights Movement, Mahalia was a **volunteer**. She sang at rallies, often praising the Reverend Martin Luther King, Jr. for preaching tolerance, love, and nonviolence. Mahalia helped in every way she could. Much of the fortune she earned from singing was donated to the civil rights cause. She began to include "freedom songs" at all her concerts. Mahalia gave money to needy but talented young people. She wanted to ensure that other students would have educational opportunities that she wished had been available for her. She demonstrated her true Christian spirit by helping whites as well as blacks. Mahalia often donated all the concert **proceeds** to charities. In August 1963, during the March on Washington, Mahalia sang just before Dr. King delivered his "I Have a Dream" speech, in which he foresaw a day when all people would be treated as equals in our country. Mahalia toured the Holy Land and saw the birthplace of Jesus Christ. Her inspirational singing touched Christians, Jews, and Arabs alike in Jerusalem.

Later in life, Mahalia's body grew more and more tired after performances, and she even had to rest in hospitals from time to time. Doctors warned her to slow down and not make long trips abroad. Still, she flew overseas for Thanksgiving in 1971 to entertain our soldiers stationed in Germany. She collapsed on stage and was rushed to a hospital. Mahalia thought she would rest better at home. She was flown back to Chicago and was admitted to Little Company of Mary Hospital. Well-wishers inquiring about Mahalia inundated the hospital switchboard. Many people sent flowers, and still more came to visit her. Mahalia died on Thursday, January 27, 1972. Her tired, loving heart had given out at last. Mahalia's voice and kind, unselfish ways "made life more beautiful and joyous for us all," as one of her millions of fans and admirers said at her funeral. Mahalia's autobiography is *Movin' On*. It was published in 1966. Her beautiful, spiritual voice lives on for posterity in her many recordings.

Activity 1

(1) Students may check a local library or music store. There are several cassettes and CDs that may be available such as *The Best of Mahalia Jackson*. Her music is also available online at Spotify and YouTube.

(2) Students may also check a local library or bookstore for the cookbook she wrote, *Mahalia Jackson Cooks Soul*. Her authentic recipes come from the days young Mahalia learned to cook in her aunt Duke's kitchen.

(3) Students would enjoy having a soul food fest while listening to Mahalia's songs.

Activity 2

Mahalia's favorite Bible verse was "Make a joyful noise unto God, all ye lands" from Psalm 66. Mahalia saw this as her mission in life.

(1) Choose a Bible verse that relates to your outlook on life.

(2) Copy it and explain what it means to you.

Match vocabulary words with definitions

Use a dictionary to match definitions for the words, as used in the context of the story.

1. debut (noun)
2. castoffs (noun)
3. volunteer (noun)
4. proceeds (noun)
5. gospel music (noun)

____(a) the profits or returns from a sale or other business transaction

____(b) a person who offers his or her services for some purpose or undertaking without charging a fee

____(c) music that deals with the life of Jesus Christ and his teachings

____(d) the first public appearance on stage

____(e) garments discarded or rejected

Answer questions in complete sentences

1. Why should Mahalia Jackson be remembered?

   _____

   _____

   _____

2. Describe some of the difficulties Mahalia faced as a child.

   _____

   _____

   _____

3. Why did Mahalia decline offers to sing with many famous black entertainers and bands?

   _____

   _____

   _____

4. Describe some of the ways Mahalia was generous with her talent and money.

_____

_____

_____

Princess Kaiulani: The Princess Who Was to Become Queen

BELLS RANG OUT from church steeples and cannons were fired off all over Hawaii when a beautiful little baby girl was born on October 16, 1875. She was **christened** Princess Victoria Kawekiu Kaiulani Kalaninuiahilapalapa Lunalilo Cleghorn. The tiny princess was simply called Kaiulani, which means "the royal sacred one" in Hawaiian.

Kaiulani was the last of royal birth in Hawaii. She was to be the new queen when she became an adult. All her life the princess was groomed for the important job. None of the princess' aunts or uncles had children of their own. Therefore, Kaiulani was to be the next queen. Her aunt Princess Ruth gave her ten acres in Waikiki as a christening gift. Ruth was one of her godmothers. Kaiulani's father was a native of Scotland named Archibald Cleghorn, and her mother was Princess Miriam Likelike, a royal Hawaiian. Her uncle King Kalakaua made Archibald governor of the Island of Oahu.

Archibald built his family a new family home on the christening gift acreage. Fresh breezes and beautiful flowers surrounded it. The family called their new home Ainahan, which means "the cool place." Today, the Princess Kaiulani Hotel is very near the original homesite. Kaiulani's favorite place to play was under a big **banyan** tree in the front yard. Her father had planted it as a birthday present. She also had a white pony named Fairy, whom she loved. She often swam and surfed in the ocean in front of her home. Kaiulani attended St. Andrews Church with her parents every Sunday. She enjoyed the carriage ride to and from church. The little princess was loved and adored by all, yet she never showed signs of being spoiled or self-centered. She was sweet, good natured, and thoughtful her entire life.

When Kaiulani was eleven years old, her mother became very ill and died. Just before Princess Miriam died, she foretold the future, saying that Kaiulani would go far from her homeland, be gone a long time, and never marry and never rule Hawaii. The young princess and her father were very sad at the passing of Princess Miriam.

When Kaiulani was fourteen, her father and aunt Ruth decided it was time for the princess to begin preparing for the day when she would become queen. It was decided that she should attend Great Harrowden Hall, a boarding school for daughters of rich and royal families located in England. Before Kaiulani left, she and a tall Scotsman named Robert Louis Stevenson became friends. The princess was sad about having to leave her family and home. The Scotsman told her stories about England. This made Kaiulani less sad and more hopeful for the future. Stevenson wrote a poem uniquely for Kaiulani.

> Forth from her land to mine she goes,
> The Island maid, the Island rose,
> Light of heart and bright of face,
> The daughter of a double race.
> Her islands here in Southern sun
> Shall mourn their Kaiulani gone,
> And I, in her dear banyan's shade,
> Look vainly for my little maid.

But our Scots island far away
Shall glitter with unwonted day,
And cast for once their tempests by
To smile in Kaiulani's eye.

Father traveled on the ship with her to San Francisco then returned home to Hawaii. The princess traveled on across the United States and across the Atlantic Ocean with her *kahu*, or nanny.

At Harrowden, Kaiulani was an excellent student and earned the love and respect of professors and students alike. The princess came to enjoy her eight-year stay in England. She became easily well-known in the many royal courts of Europe by the beautiful bright yellow gown she wore to official affairs.

Kaiulani had been in England for two years when her uncle King Kalakaua died. The princess was now age sixteen. Queen Liliuokalani, who had no children, said that Kaiulani would soon be the new queen. Two years later, foreign businessmen in Hawaii forced the queen to give up the throne. They set up their own government and laws for Hawaii. Kaiulani traveled to Washington, DC, with her guardian Mr. Theo Davies to appeal to President Grover Cleveland to intervene in the crisis on behalf of the native Hawaiian people. President Cleveland tried to help but refused to send American troops to block the white **haoles** revolution. He tried to prevent Hawaii's **annexation** to the US as long as possible but failed. Hawaiian counter-revolutionaries planned to storm Honolulu, but a spy exposed them, and their plans were thwarted. The queen was forced to sign an agreement to **abdicate** her throne. She was tried for treason and sentenced to five years of hard labor.

Young Kaiulani felt compelled to return to her homeland and to her people. She was heartbroken when she witnessed the broken spirit and sad faces of the native Hawaiians. When Cleveland left office, Congress annexed Hawaii. Life was never really happy for the princess again. When she was twenty-three, she attended the wedding of her friend Eva Parker of Parker Ranch on the big island of Hawaii. The wedding festivities lasted past Christmas. Princess Kaiulani went horseback riding in the rain with friends and caught a high fever, becoming gravely ill. Doctors said she had developed inflammatory rheumatism. For weeks she drifted in and out of consciousness. She never recovered.

Princess Kaiulani died on March 6, 1899. The casket that bore her body was brought to the church on an army caisson. A series of elderly Hawaiian women chanted a death wail, one after another as each tired. Three days later, the casket was carried on the caisson along King Street and Nuuanu Avenue to the Cleghorn family mausoleum. Guns boomed as the princess was laid to rest. Guns had boomed twenty-three years earlier, announcing a joyous occasion: the birth of the beloved princess. The second time the guns were fired for Kaiulani was a very sad day indeed. Her death marked the end of the royal line of native Hawaiians and the end of a long era in Hawaiian history. Many people mourned her passing.

Activity

Kaiulani loved the tropical flowers of Hawaii. Create tropical flower note cards. Supplies needed for each card: sturdy paper or cardstock, several colors of tissue paper, glue stick, and green crayon or felt-tip pen.

(1) Fold paper/cardstock in half to make card.

(2) Cut three (for single blossoms) or six (for double blossoms) three-inch circles from tissue paper.

(3) Using a glue stick, put dabs of glue in three spots on card where you wish to place your blossoms.

(4) Using your index finger, twist single or double circles of tissue paper over the end of your finger.

(5) Press the underside center of each blossom onto sticky spots of paper/cardstock.

(6) Draw stems and leaves with green crayon or pen to complete the flowers.

(7) After blossoms dry, write a message inside card.

You may use contrasting colors for double blossoms and a bit of glitter glue in flower centers.

Match vocabulary words with definitions

Use a dictionary to match definitions for the words below, as used in the context of the story.

1. christened (verb)

2. banyan (noun)

3. haoles (noun)

4. abdicate (verb)

5. annexation (noun)

  ____(a) the act of adding something, especially territory

  ____(b) to formally give up or relinquish one's throne

  ____(c) an East Indian fig tree whose branches send out roots to the ground, sometimes causing the tree to spread over a wide area

  ____(d) to give a child a name at the time of Christian baptism

  ____(e) non-Polynesians, non-native Hawaiians

Answer questions in complete sentences

1. Why should Princess Kaiulani be remembered?

  _____

  _____

  _____

2. What did the dying Princess Miriam predict about her daughter's future that came true?

  _____

  _____

  _____

3. How did Kaiulani prepare for her future as Hawaii's next queen?

   _____

   _____

   _____

4. Why was the end of the young princess' short life so sad?

   _____

   _____

   _____

Juliette Gordon Low: Founder of American Girl Scouts

JULIETTE GORDON WAS born on October 3, 1860 in Savannah, Georgia. When she was a baby, the Civil War broke out, turning life in Georgia upside-down. Her father became a rebel soldier and was concerned for his young family, which included older sister Nellie and their mother. He had them relocated in Chicago to live with relatives and wait out the war in safety. Juliette was soon nicknamed Daisy. It was a name that would be used for a certain age group of Girl Scouts years in the future. Her grandmother told her stories about her great-grandmother Eleanor Lytle Kinzie, who had been captured by the Seneca Indians as a child and became friends with them even after returning to her family. They called her Little-Ship-Under-Full-Sail because she was so **determined**. Young Daisy grew up with many of the same character traits. She liked adventure, and she was determined. Once at a taffy pull, her cousin remarked that her hair was the same warm brown color as the taffy. Daisy decided to braid some taffy into her hair, thinking no one would notice since her hair color was identical to the taffy. Her mother noticed, gave her a dreadful scolding, and proceeded to cut the taffy out with a pair of scissors!

In time, the family came to also include younger sisters Alice and Mabel and younger brothers Willy and Arthur. Fun, carefree summers after the war were spent with brothers and sisters and cousins at an aunt's plantation home called Etowah Cliffs. When Juliette was away at boarding school in New York City, her little sister Alice died of **scarlet fever**. Juliette said she missed Alice even more than she knew she could.

At age twenty-two, Juliette set out to see the world. She started with England, staying with family friends, the Lows, which included girls near her age, Hattie and Amy. She fell in love with their brother Willy, marrying him several years later. Juliette developed a severe ear infection and urged her doctor to try an experimental silver nitrate treatment she had read about in a newspaper article. The doctor was **apprehensive**, but Juliette insisted. The treatment made her very sick and caused a marked hearing loss in that ear. A freak accident on Juliette's wedding day caused her to lose most of the hearing in her good ear. In the time-honored tradition, well-wishers threw rice at the happy couple. One tiny grain of rice lodged deep inside her ear. It became infected and permanently caused the hearing loss. Keeping her spirits up, Juliette and Willy entertained friends with parties while living in England. Juliette continued to travel, visiting France, India, and Egypt. She took her dogs and pet parrot Polly Poon along on these adventures.

When the Spanish-American War began, Juliette returned to the United States to assist her mother, who was organizing a hospital in Miami, Florida. This hospital was for soldiers who had become ill with typhoid fever. With her can-do attitude, Juliette secured food and milk from area farmers for the patients.

When Juliette returned to England, her husband was ill. He died in 1905. Juliette was very sad and started looking for a new project in which to **channel** her energy. Her friend

Sir Robert Baden-Powell and his sister Agnes had started Boys Scouting and Girl Guides in England. They taught outdoor and survival skills: tracking, exploring, first aid, map reading, signaling, knot tying, and cooking to children.

Juliette returned to America very excited to launch scouting in her homeland. She started in Savannah by calling on an old friend, Nina Pope. Next, she traveled from city to city to set up troops and find leaders. Her efforts paid off, and scouting caught on all across the nation. The first American Girl Scouts camp was on Lookout Mountain in Georgia. Juliette was honored by having it named after her: Camp Juliette Low.

After World War I, Juliette set up World Camps where scouts and guides from all over the world could meet and promote **goodwill** and peace. This would be done by showing people that humans everywhere are more alike than different and could work cooperatively to create harmony. There was a sincere, though probably very naïve, view that World War I was "the war to end all wars." Many people were genuinely involved in efforts to promote world peace.

Some of Juliette's favorite memories were of the World Camp of 1926 in New York. By this time, Juliette was ill with cancer. Although she was experiencing pain with her illness, she really enjoyed the camp and all that it represented. She died in 1927 at age sixty-six.

Juliette's good works were honored. The Juliette Low World Friendship Fund was started soon after her death to honor her hopes for world friendship and peace. A United States federal building, a postage stamp, and ship were all named for her! A sculpture of Juliette was placed at the Georgia State Capitol. March 12 is celebrated as the Girl Scouts birthday because on that day in 1912, Juliette met with the first troop of American Girl Scouts in Savannah.

Activity 1

Play Girl Scout Games. A long list of international games are detailed in the Girl Scout's handbook, such as Rabbit with a House from Brazil, Jan-Ken-Pon from Japan, Mr. Bear from Sweden, Hawk and Hens from Zimbabwe, Sheep and Hyena from Sudan, Kim's Game from England, and Red Light, Green Light from the USA.

Activity 2

For many years now, Girl Scouts sell a number of different varieties of cookies to raise funds.

(1) Students may make suggestions for a new variety of cookie, bringing in home-baked samples, sampling the cookies, and voting for their favorite cookie. The cookie with the most votes will be considered the class favorite.

(2) Class may not be able to influence Girl Scouts to include their favorite, but it could be fun to write to the national headquarters at 30 East 33rd St., New York, NY, 10022, and see the response. At the very least, the class will enjoy sampling all the cookies!

Match vocabulary words with definitions

Use a dictionary to match definitions for the words below, as used in the context of the story.

1. determined (adjective)

2. scarlet fever (noun)

3. apprehensive (adjective)

4. channel (verb)

5. goodwill (noun)

_____(a) to direct toward or through some particular course

_____(b) anxious, uneasy, fearful

_____(c) benevolence; a cheerful or friendly disposition

_____(d) a contagious disease caused by streptococcus and characterized by red eruptions on the skin

_____(e) resolute, unwaveringly decided, staunch

Answer questions in complete sentences

1. Why should Juliette Gordon Low be remembered?

2. How did the Civil War change young Juliette's life?

3. How did Juliette lose most of her hearing?

4. What kind of skills did Girl Scouts learn in the early days of scouting?

_____

_____

_____

Wilma Mankiller: Chief of the Cherokee

WILMA MANKILLER WAS born on November 18, 1945 in Tehlequah, Oklahoma, to a mother of Dutch-Irish **descent** and a father who was a full-blooded Cherokee Indian. Wilma grew up with six brothers and four sisters in extreme poverty. Their home had no electricity or plumbing, yet they were a loving, happy family. Her family raised strawberries as their livelihood.

Two events changed Wilma's life dramatically. After a two-year **drought**, all the strawberry plants died. Then the federal government moved Indians off their rural farms and ranches and into cities beginning in 1957. This was the Bureau of Indian Affairs Relocation Program. Supposedly the **exodus** to the cities would offer Indians more opportunities for better jobs and homes. This mainstreaming actually created more problems for Indians. In San Francisco Wilma's family could no longer grow their own food. Just to cover bare living expenses in the city, both parents had to work. Before long, Wilma's oldest brother quit school to help his parents make a living.

In time, Wilma adjusted to urban life. After completing high school, she returned to Oklahoma and earned a bachelor's degree in social work at Flaming Rainbow University. Wilma entered Skyline College to do graduate work. Next, she enrolled in San Francisco State University to continue graduate work, where she met and married a student from Ecuador named Hector Hugo Olaya. A year later they became the parents of Felicia, born in 1964. The couple's second daughter, Gina, was born in 1966. In 1969 Native American students took control of Alcatraz Island to draw attention to Indian problems. This was a **wake-up call** for the activist in Wilma, who decided to become active in social issues affecting Indians. Wilma went back to college to study sociology and community development. She worked as Native American program coordinator with the Oakland Public Schools.

Yearning for the stability of her childhood surroundings, Wilma moved with her daughters back to Oklahoma in 1976. By then it was clear that she and her husband had different priorities, so they ended their marriage. Hector adhered to the traditional view that a woman's place was only in the home. Wilma felt strongly that she should pursue issues and actions to improve the lives of the Cherokee. One by one her brothers and sisters moved home also. Wilma felt happier and more secure back in Oklahoma.

Once home in Oklahoma, Wilma became acutely aware of many problems and her desire to remedy them. Tahlequah was headquarters for the Cherokee Nation. Wilma wrote grant applications to obtain federal funds for various tribal programs. She thought Indians could solve their own problems better than the government could. The Cherokee people originally lived in Georgia, South Carolina, North Carolina, and Tennessee. But in 1838 President Andrew Jackson forced their exodus to northeastern Oklahoma 1,200 miles away. Of the sixteen thousand Indians who began the trip, four thousand died on the Trail of Tears. Once in Oklahoma, the relocated

Indians drew up a constitution, built roads and schools, and settled onto farms and ranches. They developed a thriving community. When the Civil War erupted, some Cherokee supported the South, and some supported the North. After the war, more whites continued moving westward and, at times, onto Indian lands. In 1907 the federal government took the land away from the Indians, created the state of Oklahoma, and dissolved the Cherokee Nation. In 1946 the government allowed the Cherokee to reorganize. They set up health services, job-training centers, and Cherokee schools to teach the old ways. All that changed with the move to the cities during the 1950s.

When Wilma returned to her home, she wanted to help the Cherokee regain control of their lives. The biggest concern was better homes with running water. She helped teach Indians how to build and repair their own homes and how to install water systems.

Chief Ross Swimmer recognized Wilma's organizational skills. By 1979 Wilma was tribal planner and program development specialist. She took more classes, this time at the University of Arkansas. On her way home from school one day, she suffered broken legs and ribs, as well as severe facial injuries, in a bad auto accident that required seventeen surgical procedures to heal her. By 1981 she was back on the job. In 1983 Chief Swimmer asked her to become his deputy chief. In 1985 President Ronald Reagan appointed Swimmer the director of the Bureau of Indian Affairs. Wilma was the natural choice for chief of the Cherokee Nation. She won the election with over 56% of the votes. Wilma was so proud! She was the first female **chief** in modern times. Before Europeans came to America, women shared tribal power with men. Children belonged to the mother's family, not the father's. So having a woman leader was both progressive and a return to the old ways. In 1986 Wilma married Charlie Soap. A fellow Cherokee, Charlie had worked with Wilma on Indian issues. Wilma handsomely won her reelection. In the ten years she was chief, Wilma handled a budget that grew from $55 to $75 million dollars. She was responsible for matters that concerned 120,000 Cherokee people.

Wilma declined to run for a third term due to health problems. From early adulthood, she had suffered from an inherited kidney ailment that killed her beloved father. Wilma endured two kidney transplants. Her brother Donald was the donor for the first surgery. In 1995 Wilma was diagnosed with breast cancer. With treatment, it went into remission. In March 2010 she was ill with pancreatic cancer, which took her life on April 6 of that year. Her memorial at the Cherokee National Cultural Grounds was attended by 1,200 people. Wilma's hard work and dedication have earned her many awards and honors. The Oklahoma Federation of Women chose her as American Indian Woman of the Year in 1986. She was *Ms Magazine*'s Woman of the Year in 1987. She was honored with the International Women's Forum Hall of Racial Justice Award in 1992. Oklahoma's Institute of Indian Heritage honored Wilma at their annual "Spirit of the People" festival in the fall of 1994. Also in 1994 Wilma was inducted into the National Cowgirl Museum and the Hall of Fame in Fort Worth, Texas, as well as the Oklahoma Hall of Fame. In 1995 she received the Chubb Fellowship at Yale University. In 1998 Wilma was awarded the President's Medal of Freedom. This is the highest honor a citizen can receive from our government.

Wilma's book *Mankiller: A Chief and Her People* tells about her family leaving rural Oklahoma and moving to San Francisco in the mid-1950s. She also wrote *Every Day Is a Good Day: Reflections by Contemporary Indigenous Women* and *The Chief Cooks: Traditional Cherokee Recipes.* Additionally, Wilma was one of the editors of *Promoting Effective State-Tribal Relations: A Dialog* and wrote the introduction for Albert L. Hurtado's book *Reflections on American Indian History: Honoring the Past, Building a Future.*

When asked about her unusual last name, Wilma explained that it had been a title of an ancestor. Mankiller was the name given the protector of the village. The family was so proud of the title that it was agreed it would be their family name!

Activity 1

(1) Students think about what in their community could be changed to make life better for its citizens.

(2) Students will write a paragraph identifying the problem and their ideas for a remedy.

Activity 2

Look up the Cherokee alphabet and compare it to our own. The Cherokee alphabet can be found online and in many encyclopedias.

Activity 3

Indians often have names that describe their personalities or physical attributes.

(1) Students will choose descriptive name for themselves and write them on strips of paper.

(2) The strips will be placed in a container, and the teacher will draw them out one at a time and read them aloud to the class.

(3) Students will try to guess students' identities.

(4) Students may want to use their Indian names for the rest of the day!

Match vocabulary words with definitions

Use a dictionary to match definitions of words below, as used in the context of the story.

1. drought (noun)
2. descent (noun)
3. wake-up call (noun)
4. exodus (noun)
5. chief (noun)

_____(a) the head or leader of an organization

_____(b) a period of dry weather without any rain especially injurious to crops

_____(c) a departure or emigration usually of a large number of people

_____(d) a catalyst or something that alerts or makes a situation apparently clear to someone, especially a situation that necessitates action to remedy

_____(e) lineage, derivation from an ancestor

Answer questions in complete sentences

1. Why should Wilma Mankiller be remembered?

_____

_____

_____

2. What events in Wilma's childhood greatly changed her family's life?

_____

_____

_____

3. When the Cherokee had been moved from their ancestral lands to Oklahoma, what steps did they take to improve their lives?

_____

_____

_____

4. How did Wilma become chief of the Cherokee?

_____

_____

_____

Sandra Day O'Connor: First Woman Supreme Court Justice

SANDRA DAY WAS born on March 26, 1930 in El Paso, Texas. Her parents, Harry and Ada Mae Day, lived on a cattle ranch in the southeastern corner of Arizona. The ranch was so remote that her mother journeyed to her own parents' home in Texas for the birth of her child. Sandra loved growing up in Arizona on the Lazy B Ranch, always helping with whatever needed done ever since she was a tiny little girl. Being a girl was never an excuse for not doing her best, whether it was ranch chores or schoolwork. Sandra's brother was not born until she was eight years old, so Sandra's playmates were the ranch animals and wild animals. The ranch required reinvesting the money her parents made. There was little money for extras. Both parents did, however, value education. They belonged to a book-of-the-month club and subscribed to *National Geographic* and *Saturday Evening Post* magazines.

When Sandra was old enough for school, her mother, a former teacher, taught her at home. That worked well for a while, but her parents felt she needed to be with other children. The nearest school was in Lordsburg, so far away that a daily commute would require arising before dawn and getting home after dark. That was too long a day for a small child. It was decided that young Sandra would go to live with her grandparents in El Paso and attend Radford

Girl's School during the school year. Sandra loved school, her new friends, and her grandparents, but she dearly missed her parents and the ranch. Vacations were never long enough.

Her brother Alan was born when she was eight and her sister Ann when she was ten. By the end of seventh grade, Sandra insisted on coming home for eighth grade so she could spend more time with her family. Sandra managed the difficult schedule for the school year then returned to Texas for high school, where she graduated near the top of her class at age sixteen.

Sandra's only choice for college was Stanford University. This was the college her father had planned to attend as a young man. However, the death of his own father had necessitated him forgoing college to operate the family ranch. It never occurred to Sandra to apply anywhere else but Stanford University in case she was not admitted. But she was admitted because of her excellent grades and broad interests. Originally, Sandra had intended to study business and economics and then return to Arizona to run the ranch. However, she became interested in law when Professor Rathbun showed her that each person can make a difference in their world.

Sandra started Stanford Law School after only three years of college under a rule established in 1945 to help returning World War II servicemen finish college faster. The rule was open to women also, so Sandra took advantage of it. In law school she met John O'Connor, whom she married in December of 1952 on her family's ranch. The couple exchanged wedding vows in Sandra's childhood home. The barn was decorated with lots of evergreen branches. The happy couple was surrounded by family and friends and had a festive reception in the beautifully decorated barn during the Christmas season.

Even with a law degree from a top-rated school, Sandra found it difficult getting hired. She applied for many positions. In the 1950s, few firms welcomed women lawyers. Finally, Sandra was hired as a staff **attorney** for San Mateo County in Northern California. John had one more year of law school to complete. Soon after John graduated, he was drafted into the army, and the couple was sent to Frankfurt, West Germany, where John became a lawyer for the United States Army. Sandra worked as a civilian lawyer, writing legal contracts and helping distribute surplus goods after World War II. She met and became friends with a Mrs. Blankenburg, who was a one-person social service agency. Instead of becoming bitter after having lost her sixteen-year-old son in the war, she instead devoted her life to helping others. Mrs. Blankenburg was precisely the kind of person Professor Rathbun at Stanford had described when he said that one person could make positive changes in the world.

Returning to the United States, the O'Connors settled in Phoenix, Arizona, near Sandra's old college friend Diane and her husband. Sandra and John studied and passed the Arizona Bar Exam. John found a job with a law firm. Sandra had difficulty once again getting hired. Instead, she opened her own office with a young man who had studied for the **bar exam** with Sandra and John. Sandra worked on many kinds of cases. She continued to work briefly after the births of her sons, Scott, Brian, and Jay. She took off the next years to be home with her children. In her spare time, Sandra took volunteer jobs that related to children and the law, organized a legal service for poor people, wrote questions for the Arizona State Bar Exam, and worked for the Republican Party, getting local candidates of **integrity** elected. Sandra was very organized in all she did.

Later, when Sandra decided to seek paid work again, she found it was still difficult for a woman to get a job as an attorney. She kept applying for a position as an attorney with the state attorney general's office. She was finally hired as an assistant attorney general, where she tackled the problems of the Arizona State Hospital for the Mentally Ill and helped find solutions. She also worked for other state government departments, including the Welfare Department and the Treasurer's Office. When an empty seat came up in the Arizona State Senate, Sandra wanted to fill it. She was anxious to change bad laws and make new ones. The County Board of Supervisors appointed her. Sandra completed the term, and then she was elected to two more terms.

In 1972 the Arizona's Republican State Senators elected Sandra to be their leader. There were more Republicans than Democrats in the Arizona State Senate, so the Republicans were the majority, and their leader was the majority leader. That made Sandra the first woman majority leader in the whole country! Sandra was respected because she really listened to the senators' different ideas and put the ideas together in a format that would work. Sandra was also respected because she always did her homework. She studied and researched every issue very carefully. Sandra was described as tactful, but tough. She made sure laws were written correctly the first time, paying special attention to wording and punctuation so they would not be **ambiguous** and need to be redone. Many of her laws helped women, children, and the poor. That job was only a part-time position, allowing Sandra to have valuable time with her husband and sons. She and John were very involved in every aspect of their sons' lives and taught the boys love and responsibility.

In 1979 Governor Bruce Babbitt appointed Sandra to the Arizona Court of Appeals. He told the press, "She was the finest talent available—her intellectual ability and her judgment are astonishing!"

In June of 1981 President Ronald Reagan kept his campaign promise to put a woman on the Supreme Court. Sandra was at the top of a short list of qualified women submitted to the president. She was the favorite because she had experience in all three branches of the government: executive, legislative, and judicial. Sandra was confirmed **unanimously** by both houses of Congress! John and the boys were very proud of her!

Justice Sandra Day O'Connor continued to do her homework and consider every aspect of a case very carefully. She was considered the swing vote because it was difficult to predict how she would rule on any given case. Sandra tended to be most concerned in the constitutionality of a case, rather than a political agenda. She was well-respected by her colleagues. As busy as her schedule was, Sandra recognized the connection between a sound body and a sound mind. She made exercise a regular part of her day by organizing an office aerobics time each morning. Sandra and office staff donned their Workout with the Supremes T-shirts, completed their workout, and showered before beginning their workday!

Justice O'Connor's husband, John, became ill with Alzheimer's disease in 2005. She decided to retire as soon as President George W. Bush could nominate her successor.

Judge Samuel Alito was nominated and confirmed. Justice O'Connor was able to spend quality time with her husband until his death in 2009.

In retirement, Justice O'Connor has been busy from time to time with speaking engagements. She has also written four books: *Lazy B: Growing Up on a Cattle Ranch in the American Southwest* (2002), *The Majesty of the Law: Reflections of a Supreme Court Justice* (2003), *Chico* (2005), and *Finding Susie* (2009). The last two books are for children.

While visiting her old elementary school, Radford, in El Paso, Texas, Sandra told students to do their best at whatever job they are given because that would prepare them for any opportunity to come in the future. She repeated what Professor Rathbun had taught her many years ago: "The individual can make things happen."

Activity

Read the book *The True Story of the Three Little Pigs* and the traditional version to the class.

(1) Ask students to decide whom they believe, the wolf or the pig. Talk about how there are usually at least two sides to every issue.

(2) Ask students aligned in two groups to present "evidence" either for or against the wolf's claim that he was unjustly framed for murder. The wolf insists the deaths were accidents and eating the bodies was logical. This will create a lively class discussion.

(3) Conclude with students pretending they are judges and writing legal opinions of the wolf's guilt or innocence. Remind students to cite their reasons based on the evidence in the stories.

Match vocabulary words with definitions

Use a dictionary to match definitions for the words below, as used in the context of the story.

1. attorney (noun)

2. bar exam (noun)

3. integrity (noun)

4. ambiguous (adjective)

5. unanimously (adverb)

_____(a) completely in agreement

_____(b) a legal agent qualified to act for persons in legal proceedings _____(c) honesty, uprightness, soundness of and adherence to moral principles and character

_____(d) having several possible meanings or interpretations; not clear

_____(e) tests one must pass to be licensed as an attorney

Answer questions in complete sentences

1. Why should Sandra Day O'Connor be remembered?

_____

_____

_____

2. How did Sandra's parents encourage her to achieve her potential?

_____

_____

_____

3. What effect did Professor Rathbun's statement have on Sandra's education and career choice?

_____

_____

_____

4. How did Sandra successfully combine family life and a career?

_____

_____

_____

Rosa Parks: Mother of the Civil Rights Movement

Rosa Louise McCauley Parks was born in Tuskegee, Alabama, on February 4, 1913 to a young black couple. Her mother, Leona, was a schoolteacher, and her father, Sylvester, was a carpenter and homebuilder. Rosa's great-grandparents had been slaves. Her parents taught her to work hard for a living. She worked in the summer on her maternal grandparents' small farm and in nearby cotton fields. Rosa cleared weeds and picked cotton. When Rosa's parents separated, she, her mother, and brother, Sylvester, moved to her McCauley grandparents' farm.

Life for young Rosa was very different from that of white children her age. While Rosa was a child and a young woman, there were many laws that **discriminated** against people of African ancestry. "Jim Crow" laws kept whites and blacks **segregated** in public places, such as schools, restaurants, hotels, churches, and theaters. Black people could not drink from "whites only" drinking fountains or use "whites only" restrooms. On buses blacks were limited to the back seats and were often made to enter the back door of the bus. If all the front seats filled and whites were not seated, blacks were made to give up their seats. Age and physical condition carried no weight. An old or tired black person would be obligated to surrender his/her seat to any white person. The laws were unfair, but most people just suffered through the conditions.

While Rosa was a child, she attended a school for black children that only went through sixth grade and operated for only five months out of the year. Her education was clearly not equal to that of white children. Although most black students never went beyond sixth grade, Rosa then attended Industrial School for Girls in Montgomery. It was a laboratory school in the Alabama State Teachers College for Negroes School. Before Rosa finished high school, she dropped out to care for her ailing grandmother and mother.

In 1931 Rosa met a barber named Raymond Parks. They married the next year in December. Raymond was active in the Civil Rights struggle. Rosa admired her husband's integrity. She became the secretary of the Montgomery, Alabama, branch of the National Association for the Advancement of Colored People, which became known by its initials, NAACP. Raymond encouraged Rosa to complete her high school education. She enrolled and completed high school.

One day in December 1955, on her way home from her job as a department store tailor's assistant, Rosa boarded a bus on Cleveland Avenue in Montgomery. The bus driver was James Blake, who on an earlier occasion had taken Rosa's bus fare then driven off while she was made to go to the back entrance to board. On this December day, more white passengers boarded the bus at the next stop. The driver demanded that Rosa and other blacks surrender their seats to whites. Rosa was tired of being treated unjustly. She simply and quietly—but firmly—refused. The driver called the police and had Rosa **arrested.**

The unfairness of the incident caused uproar in the black communities of the city. Some people wanted to use guns to free Rosa from jail. Dr. Martin Luther King, Jr., the minister of the Dexter Avenue Baptist Church, calmed the people. He convinced them that instead of force, they could use simple economics to solve the problem. They launched a citywide **boycott** by blacks of all Montgomery buses. Losing the black riders' business cost the bus line a lot of lost income. A great number of customers of the bus service were blacks traveling from home to work and back. Although the boycott caused some inconveniences for black passengers, they knew that they would only effect change if they fully supported the boycott. Montgomery's black citizens with cars began carpooling while others walked. They refused to ride the buses as long as the discrimination persisted. The boycott worked! On November 13, 1956, after nearly a year, the Supreme Court of the United States handed down a judgment saying that segregation was unconstitutional. News reached Montgomery, and the boycott ended on December 21, 1956. Reporters interviewed Rosa. The Civil Rights Movement was building momentum. Rosa and Raymond traveled to many demonstrations and Civil Rights marches. They received frightening telephone threats. The Ku Klux Klan, a white terrorist group, threatened and often murdered blacks for no reason other than racial hatred.

Rosa's family moved to Detroit to be near her brother. She worked in the office of Congressman John Conyers, a member of the United States House of Representatives. Rosa enjoyed helping people. One of her contributions to the congressman's office was helping constituents find housing. Although their time in Detroit had many happy and rewarding times, the late 1970s brought much heartache to Rosa's life. Her husband, Raymond, died after a lengthy illness in 1977. Her brother, Sylvester, died soon after. In 1979 Rosa's mother passed away also.

In 1987 Rosa founded the Raymond and Rosa Parks Institute of Self-Development. The purpose was to help young people finish their education. Rosa and Raymond knew education was an important ingredient in fulfilling a person's potential. Education could help free people from a life of seemingly hopeless poverty and dead ends. In 1992 Rosa published her autobiography, *Rosa Parks, My Story*. The book was aimed at young readers and explained events and decisions in her life that led to her refusing to give up her bus seat in 1955. Three years later in 1995, she wrote *Quiet Strength*, a memoir explaining how faith had always been part of her life and helped her every day. Many people have called Rosa the Mother of the Civil Rights Movement. Thanks to such people as the diminutive women named Rosa, many needed laws have been passed to **empower** Americans to enjoy more personal freedoms and opportunities, clearly our birthright as Americans. Many honors, such as the Martin Luther King, Jr. Nonviolent Peace Prize, the Spingarn Medal, the Eleanor Roosevelt Woman of Courage Award, the Congressional Gold Medal, and the Presidential Medal of Freedom have been bestowed on the little seamstress turned civil rights advocate.

Rosa was diagnosed with progressive dementia in 2004 and passed away on October 24, 2005. The city buses in Detroit, Michigan, and Montgomery, Alabama, reserved their front seats with black ribbons in Rosa's honor and remained there until her burial. Rosa's remains were flown to Montgomery and taken to the St. Paul African Methodist Church by a horse-drawn hearse. She lay in repose until the next morning. Secretary of State Condoleezza Rice spoke at her service. Next, Rosa's remains were flown to Washington, DC, and then carried in a bus like the ones used in 1955 to the Capitol Rotunda. She lay in honor; over fifty thousand people passed by her casket. After a memorial in the capitol, Rosa's remains were flown back to Detroit to the Charles H. Wright Museum of African American History. She lay in repose for two days. Her funeral was held on November 2, 2005 at Greater Grace Temple Church, where services lasted seven hours. An honor guard from the Michigan National Guard laid a flag over the casket before giving it to Rosa's niece. Along the route to the cemetery, thousands of people paid their respects and released white balloons. President George W. Bush ordered all flags in Washington, DC, and all United States' public areas be flown at half-mast. The quiet little seamstress who had refused to abandon her seat and stand the rest of the bus trip modestly became the mother of the civil rights movement. Rosa's contributions then and for the rest of her life made many other people's lives much easier!

If you are ever in Montgomery, Alabama, be sure to visit the old Cleveland Avenue, now appropriately renamed Rosa Parks Boulevard!

Activity

To give students an idea of what it was like to live under segregation laws, set up a classroom scenario for a day.

(1) Draw names to distinguish which students will have "full rights" and which will have "few rights."

(2) Label items around the room as "full rights" and "few rights," such as being allowed to use the drinking fountain, pencil sharpener, encyclopedia, dictionaries, windows, paper, pencils, chalk, etc.

(3) Grant privileges to "full rights" students such as first in line, calling on them during class discussions, etc. and penalize "few rights" students by making them go to back of lines and by ignoring them during class discussions, etc.

(4) Near the end of the school day, ask "few rights" students how they feel being denied basic rights? How did they feel being treated as less than full citizens?

(5) Ask "full rights" students how did they feel being given preferential treatment?

(6) Students will write a half-page response explaining how they now feel after having been exposed to discrimination.

(7) Students will share their reactions aloud with the class.

Match vocabulary words with definitions

Use a dictionary to match definitions for the words below, as used in the context of the story.

1. discriminated (verb)

2. segregated (verb)

3. arrested (verb)

4. boycott (noun)

5. empower (verb)

____(a) separated or set apart from others because of race, religion, etc., often by force

____(b) seized a person by legal authority or warrant; taken into custody

____(c) to enable or permit, give power or authority

____(d) made a distinction in favor of or against a person or thing on the basis of the group, class, or category to which the person or thing belongs, rather than according to actual merit

____(e) the practice of abstaining from or preventing dealings with by means of intimidation or coercion

Answer questions in complete sentences

1. Why should Rosa Parks be remembered?

_____

_____

_____

2. How was Rosa's childhood different from the childhoods of white children her age?

_____

_____

_____

3. Why do you think Rosa has become known as the Mother of the Civil Rights Movement?

_____

_____

_____

4. What did Rosa do to help others achieve their goals, after her husband, Sylvester, died?

_____

_____

_____

Eleanor Roosevelt: First Lady of the World

ANNA ELEANOR ROOSEVELT was born on October 11, 1884 to a wealthy young couple. Her father, Elliott, was the brother of Theodore Roosevelt. Her mother, Anna Hall Roosevelt, had three ancestors who had signed the Declaration of Independence. When Eleanor was only two years old, her parents took her on an ocean voyage aboard the *Britannia*, which sank. Everyone was saved, but Eleanor vividly remembered the **trauma** of being dropped overboard to her father who was in a lifeboat far below. She never forgot the terror she had felt as a toddler being dropped.

Her father was very loving, calling her Golden Hair and Little Nell, but his **alcoholism** created many problems for the family. Eleanor did not understand when she was little. Her mother died from **diphtheria** in December 1892, and her brother Elliott Jr. died the next spring. Her father died in 1894 from injuries he was unable to survive from a drunken fall. Eleanor was not yet ten years old, and she had lost the three most important people in her life. She missed her father, mother, and little brother dearly. She spent the rest of her childhood being raised by her stern and strict maternal Grandmother Hall.

Eleanor wanted so much to attend school, but Grandmother Hall did not believe in educating girls. Eleanor was only allowed private tutors at home. She was not allowed to attend school. She missed being with other children. Aunt Bye, Elliott's sister, **intervened** often on Eleanor's behalf. Worried about the sad, lonely child, Aunt Bye tried to spend as much time as possible with her. Eleanor had one other relative who appreciated how she felt. Her uncle Teddy Roosevelt was as encouraging with young Eleanor and his own children as Grandmother Hall was restricting and stern. When Eleanor visited Uncle Teddy's family, she was allowed—actually encouraged—to romp and play as a child. Uncle Teddy thought children should have fun and be given wide latitude in exploring their surroundings. Some of her happiest carefree memories were with Uncle Teddy, Aunt Edie, and cousins.

When Eleanor was fifteen years old, Aunt Bye arranged for her to be sent to Allenswood, a girls' private secondary school in England. Eleanor loved the three years she spent there. With her excellent memory, she was able to memorize long poems and complete sections of books. Eleanor blossomed in the nurturing, encouraging environment. One of her teachers took the young girl on European **excursions** during school vacations.

At age eighteen Eleanor returned home and wanted to attend college, but Grandmother Hall would not allow it, saying a college education for her was not appropriate. Grandmother Hall felt that higher education for a girl was a waste of time and money. Determined to channel her energies in a positive pursuit, Eleanor devoted her days to Rivington Street Settlement House. There she helped improve conditions for the mass of immigrant poor. She enjoyed her work and became a strong force for social change.

In 1905 Eleanor married Franklin Roosevelt, a distant cousin. On her wedding day, Uncle Teddy took his deceased brother's place, walking his niece down the aisle and giving her away. Eleanor and Franklin became a couple of distinction. Over the years Eleanor's role became nationally more and more important. During her husband's four terms in office, she was his eyes, ears, and legs after Franklin contracted polio. She wrote several books, including *It's Up to the Women* in 1933 and *This I Remember* in 1949, as well as a daily newspaper column called "My Day." Eleanor spoke out for civil rights and for national unity and against social injustice. When the Daughters of the American Revolution refused to allow black singer Marian Anderson to perform for them, Eleanor arranged for a special free Easter Sunday concert in front of the Lincoln Memorial open to everyone. It was a huge success. Eleanor also resigned from the DAR organization on principle.

Eleanor was one of the most admired and hardworking First Ladies ever. After World War II and the formation of the United Nations, President Truman asked Eleanor to chair the committee that drafted the United Nations Universal Declaration of Human Rights. Eleanor soon became known as First Lady of the World. In some of the most trying and challenging times of our country's history, Eleanor raised her five children while being fully involved in her husband's lengthy political career. After a long and useful life, Eleanor died on November 7, 1962. Former presidents Truman and Eisenhower, as well as the sitting president, John F. Kennedy and his wife, Jackie, attended her funeral. Adlai E. Stevenson, statesman and diplomat, spoke and praised Eleanor saying, "She would rather light a candle than curse the darkness, and her glow has warmed the world."

Eleanor was buried beside her husband in the rose garden of their Hyde Park estate in New York. In Washington, DC, a large statue honoring Eleanor is situated near one for her husband. The Eleanor Roosevelt Memorial is located in Riverside Park of the Manhattan Borough in New York City. It was dedicated on October 5, 1996. It features a plaque detailing Eleanor's many accomplishments and a beautiful statue of this thoughtful advocate, writer, humanitarian, and former American First Lady, who was also respectfully remembered as the First Lady of the World.

Activity 1

In modern times, the spouse of the president has had a pet project. Lady Bird Johnson's was "Keeping America Beautiful," Nancy Reagan's was "Just Say No" to drugs, and Barbara Bush's was literacy.

(1) Students decide what their special projects would be if someday in the future they become the husband or wife of an American president.

(2) Students will make posters to promote their pet projects.

(3) Posters will be displayed in the classroom, a school hallway, or on bulletin boards.

Activity 2

Eleanor grew up feeling self-conscious about her plain looks. Her mother and aunts had been considered great beauties. Eleanor considered herself an ugly duckling. Later in life she came to understand that a person's inward beauty (good character) was more important. Eleanor once said, "No one can make you feel inferior without your consent!"

(1) What do you think she meant?

(2) Write a short paragraph explaining why you agree or disagree with Eleanor's statement.

Match vocabulary words with definitions

Use a dictionary to match definitions for the words below, as used in the context of the story.

1. trauma (noun)
2. alcoholism (noun)
3. diphtheria (noun)
4. excursions (noun)
5. intervened (verb)

_____(a) brief pleasure trips

_____(b) came in or between in order to stop, settle, or modify something

_____(c) a startling experience which has a lasting emotional effect; a shock

_____(d) a contagious, sometimes fatal disease that produces a toxin causing inflammation of the heart and nervous system

_____(e) a complex disease due to the excessive or compulsive consumption of alcohol often leading to a complex chronic psychological and nutritional disorder

Answer questions in complete sentences

1. Why should Eleanor Roosevelt be remembered?

_____

_____

_____

2. What traumas and unhappiness did Eleanor endure as a child and teenager?

_____

_____

_____

3. How did Eleanor channel her interests and energies after she was denied the opportunity to attend college?

_____

_____

_____

4. Why did Eleanor become known as the First Lady of the World?

_____

_____

_____

Annie Sullivan: Extraordinary Teacher of Helen Keller

NEARLY EVERYONE HAS heard the story of Helen Keller and her triumph over obstacles. However, fewer people know the story of her teacher, Annie Sullivan, whose life story is also very remarkable. This is not surprising because Annie remained a modest person, downplaying her own outstanding successes her entire life.

Annie Sullivan was born Johanna Mansfield Sullivan on April 14, 1866 in Fielding Hills, Massachusetts. Her parents called her Annie from the very beginning. Thomas and Alice Sullivan were recent immigrants from a life of starvation and poverty in Ireland, where crops had failed for twenty years. In Massachusetts, Thomas found work as a farm laborer. For a while the family was able to make ends meet and was happy.

With the addition of two more children, Jimmy and Mary, the Sullivan's **meager** income was insufficient to sustain the family. Out of frustration, Thomas began to drink alcohol. Alice became weak and sickly, and it was soon determined that she suffered from tuberculosis. Little Jimmy had been born with a birth defect that made his hip malformed and caused walking to be painful for him. At about the same time, young Annie began having trouble with her eyes. Painful lumps appeared inside her eyelids. The more she rubbed them, the more painful the condition grew. Thomas and Alice took her to many doctors in the area, but none of the doctors could really help the child. Annie had a **chronic** condition known as trachoma. In those days, the condition was viewed as a filthy disease of slum dwellers.

Annie began to act out in bratty behavior in her childlike attempts for more attention from her parents. The demands of the family exhausted what little energy poor, weak Alice could muster. Thomas, feeling powerless to help his ailing and impoverished family, began to drink heavily and was less responsive to his children. When Alice died, relatives split up the little family. Thomas was not even consulted. Relatives did not think a drunken father was capable of raising his own children. Baby Mary, who was healthy, was quickly adopted by an aunt. Nobody really wanted Annie or Jimmy. Finally they were sent to live with the most prosperous aunt and uncle in the family. This aunt and uncle had children of their own and did not want the sickly children. They took them in because they felt obligated to do so. From the beginning of their stay, Annie sensed that she and Jimmy were considered unwanted burdens, so she continued to misbehave out of frustration. As Christmas approached, Annie told the aunt and uncle about a doll she wanted badly. When the family opened their Christmas gifts, the very same doll that Annie longed for was given to her cousin. Annie and Jimmy each received a gift, but Annie felt slighted that her wishes had been ignored and the beautiful doll presented to someone else. That was the last straw for the little girl who had known nothing but heartache and disappointment. Annie threw a huge tantrum and smashed everything under the Christmas tree! This incident gave the aunt and uncle the excuse they had been looking for to be rid of the two unwanted children.

Annie and Jimmy were sent to the state almshouse (poorhouse) at Tewsbury. This place was bleak, cold, and depressing. It certainly was not a place suitable for children. Most of the other residents were adults who ignored or disliked children. It was made clear to Annie that she must assume care of little Jimmy, or he would be placed in a different section of the place and she would never see him again. Although Annie was not yet ten years old, she took on the role of mother/protector of her beloved little brother. There was one resident who did befriend the children. Maggie Carroll was an arthritic woman who read to Annie, and in turn Annie would help assist Maggie in her limited mobility. Annie had desperately wanted to attend school for as long as she could remember. She found books fascinating. The cruel aunt who had turned the children out ridiculed the little girl, saying, "With those eyes, you will never read!" Life at Tewsbury was somewhat bearable until Jimmy's condition grew gravely worse and he died. This was probably the lowest point of Annie's life. Everyone she loved and everyone who loved her was gone. Annie was sad and miserable. She wanted more than ever to escape from Tewsbury.

In time, a priest named Father Barbara took Annie out of the almshouse and to a hospital, where a doctor believed he could surgically restore her eyesight. By this time, Annie's vision had deteriorated to near-blindness. After several operations, her eyesight remained the same. Annie explained to Father Barbara how desperately she wanted to attend school. In time she was allowed to attend the Perkins Institute for the Blind as a charity case. At first, when anyone hurt Annie's feelings, she reacted to the frustration in the only way she knew how—throwing tantrums! After a while, Annie began to trust one kind teacher, Miss Moore. She began to **emulate** her teacher's thoughtful behavior. This marked a new beginning for Annie. She learned to read by a raised letter system called Braille and by a manual method where the letters are formed in the palm of the hand. Annie excelled in her studies and graduated **valedictorian**.

After graduating, Annie found a job as a maid in a rooming house. One of the boarders had a friend, Dr. Bradford, who after several more operations, partially restored Annie's vision. Returning to Perkins Institute, Annie was at first kept busy running errands and finally given a limited teaching position.

One day the school director received a letter from a family in Alabama whose young daughter was deaf, mute, and blind. She could not hear, speak, or see. The child had progressed normally until the age of nineteen months, when an illness robbed her of sight and hearing. Little Helen was isolated in a dark, silent world. The family wrote to Perkins, seeking a **governess** to teach their handicapped child. The school director immediately thought Annie would make an appropriate governess, considering the obstacles she herself had overcome. Annie was offered the job. She did not want to move to rural Alabama, much preferring to stay in a busy, active city. Having few options, however, Annie accepted the position.

Arriving at the Keller home on March 3, 1887, Annie found the situation even more daunting than she could have imagined. In addition to teaching the six-year-old, she would first need to civilize the child! Out of pity for her limitations, the family had coddled Helen, spoiling her and allowing the child to do as she pleased. The child threw tantrums any time someone failed to immediately respond to her demands. Helen was accustomed to grabbing food with her bare hands from everyone's plates during meals. She was essentially an undisciplined wild animal with no manners whatsoever!

Annie persuaded the parents to give her two weeks alone with Helen and to not interfere no matter how much Helen protested. Annie isolated herself with her little charge in the family's guest cottage. The determined governess persisted in her plan to civilize the little tyrant throughout Helen's many temper tantrums. The breakthrough came with a combination of strength and kindness. While Annie and Helen were outside pumping water, the feel of the water trickling over her hands fascinated Helen. She seemed to want to know what it was. Annie taught Helen to sign W-A-T-E-R with the manual alphabet she had been teaching the child. Helen soon was signing not only water, but many words and connecting the words to objects. The Keller family was thrilled! Annie's patience and persistence came from her own memories of being a hurting, frustrated, lonely child and the many kindnesses Miss Moore had shown her.

By August, after less than six months of tutoring, Helen had learned 625 words! By October, she was writing letters in the Braille method to pen pals at Perkins Institute. By June of 1888, Helen was invited to participate in commencement exercises at Perkins because of her amazing progress. Annie and Helen traveled to Massachusetts for the graduation. They were invited to stay on at the school, Helen as a student and Annie as a teacher. Annie declined, saying that the school was too small a world for Helen. By spring of 1890, Helen had learned to talk with her voice.

This was a tremendous accomplishment for someone who had not heard anything since she was nineteen months old. Helen was only the second blind-deaf person in recorded history to achieve this difficult task.

Helen became more and more famous as she reached each new goal. Annie modestly stayed in the background but was there helping Helen every step of the way. At age twelve, Helen proudly announced, "I have decided to go to college. And the one I want to go to is Harvard!" In the fall of 1900, Helen became a freshman at Radcliffe College, the women's equivalent of Harvard. At the time Harvard was an all-male school. Helen graduated cum laude, which means "with honors," four years later. Annie stayed on as Helen's companion over the years but modestly shied away from interviews, not wanting any recognition for herself. The teacher insisted that the student deserved all the credit for her progress. Helen became a writer of books and magazine articles about her life and the problems of being deaf and blind. The two friends toured the United States, giving talks to help people understand handicaps.

In 1905, at the age of thirty-nine, Annie married John Macy, a Harvard English professor who was also a literary critic. Annie and John met while he helped Helen edit her autobiography. Annie, John, and Helen all lived in the same house until the Macys separated in 1912.

By the 1920s, Annie's eyesight and energy were both failing. A secretary, Polly Thomason, was hired for Helen. The three women lived together in the same house. Financially, Annie was struggling. Hoping to earn some money, she starred as herself in the first film about the remarkable story of her and Helen's successes. The film, *Deliverance*, unfortunately failed miserably as a money-maker. Annie and Helen then toured the country in the vaudeville circuit, continuing to share their story with the nation for many years. Most of Annie's vision was gone by the end of the 1920s. In constant pain in one eye, she opted to have that eye removed. This allowed some relief from the pain.

On October 19, 1936 Johanna Mansfield Sullivan Macy died with Helen holding her hand in their Forest Hills, New York, home. At Annie's funeral, Bishop James E. Freeman praised Annie:

> Among the great teachers of all time she occupies
> a commanding and conspicuous place ... The touch
> of her hand did more than illuminate the pathway of
> a clouded mind; it literally emancipated a soul.

Annie's final resting place was at the National Cathedral in Washington, DC, where her ashes were laid.

Helen could have given up without her beloved teacher at her side, but every time she was about to give in to self-pity, a little silent voice would disrupt her thoughts: "Teacher would not like that, Helen!" Annie's student continued to be productive. She lectured throughout the world, using her life experiences as inspiration to other handicapped people. She visited wounded veterans in US hospitals after World War II. She continued writing until the late 1950s. If not for the love and unselfishness of Annie Sullivan, Helen most certainly would have lived out her life in dark, silent loneliness. Annie had learned well the lessons of her beloved teacher, Miss Moore, and truly made Helen Keller's life remarkable.

Eventually, Annie and Helen's story was told successfully. *The Miracle Worker* was first a play and then a movie after William Gibson wrote the screenplay. The film was so popular and successful that it was nominated for an Academy Award for Best Adapted Screenplay for 1963. Sixteen-year-old Patty Duke won the Best Supporting Actress Academy Award for her portrayal of Helen Keller. The film earned Anne Bancroft the Best Actress Academy Award for her portrayal of Annie Sullivan.

Activity

For this activity, you will need for each student:

(1) A copy of the Braille alphabet (available in most encyclopedia sets). Students will need this to write their message and to decipher their classmate's message.

(2) A sturdy piece of 8 1/2-by-11-inch cardstock.

(3) A large safety pin (at least two inches long for the pin to be large enough to make strong protruding Braille letters that can be felt with fingertips).

Directions/instructions:

(1) By poking the safety pin through the <u>back side</u> of the cardstock, each student will write a short message in Braille, doing so right to left. This message can be read with fingers on the <u>front side</u> of cardstock in a left to right, top to bottom reading pattern, just like visual reading.

(2) Using a pencil or pen, each student will then write their message on the back side of their cardstock.

(3) Each student will exchange their cardstock message with a classmate to decode. The classmate will try to "read" Braille with their fingers and then write with pencil or pen below the Braille message what they think the message says.

(4) Each classmate may now check their response with the correct message on the back of the cardstock.

This activity should help students appreciate the accomplishments of people who, with limited or no vision, have learned to read and write in Braille!

Match vocabulary words with definitions

Use a dictionary to match definitions for the words below, as used in the context of the story.

1. meager (adjective)
2. chronic (adjective)
3. emulate (verb)
4. governess (noun)
5. valedictorian (noun)

_____(a) to imitate with effort to equal or surpass

_____(b) having a long duration and frequent recurrence

_____(c) a woman employed to take charge of a child's education and upbringing

_____(d) poor, inadequate, deficient in amount

_____(e) a student, usually the one ranking academically highest in the graduating class, who also delivers the farewell speech at the graduation ceremony

Answer questions in complete sentences

1. Why should Annie Sullivan be remembered?

   _____

   _____

   _____

2. What traumas in her childhood helped shape Annie's personal strengths?

   _____

   _____

   _____

3. Why was Annie well-suited to be Helen's teacher?

   _____

   _____

   _____

4. What evidence shows that Annie was modest about her own accomplishments in teaching Helen?

   _____

   _____

   _____

Margaret Thatcher: First Woman Prime Minister of Great Britain

MARGARET ROBERTS THATCHER was born October 13, 1925 in Grantham, England, one hundred miles north of London. She was the firstborn child of Alfred and Beatrice Roberts. Margaret's mother was a seamstress. Her father was a grocer who wanted to be a teacher. He loved school but had found it necessary to interrupt his own education so that he could work to help support his parents and six brothers and sisters. Alfred valued education and encouraged Margaret and her sister to read and discuss biographies. She was an excellent student, but Margaret always found time to work in the family grocery store. The family lived in a modest apartment above the store.

Because Margaret's parents placed high value on education, they lived modestly in order to afford good schools for the girls. Margaret attended Huntingtower Road Primary School from the time she was five to ten years old. She took her studies very seriously and often spent two to three hours each night on homework. Margaret was very involved in sports and also on the debating team. At age eleven, Margaret won a medal in a speech contest. She often said that her father was the biggest influence in her life. He encouraged her to think for herself and always do her best. Margaret's quiet hometown, Grantham, had seen much history. Charles Dickens stayed at the George Hotel and even mentioned it in his book *Nicholas Nickelby*. Isaac Newton attended King's School. During World War II, the British Manufacture and Research Company was the most bombed factory in Britain.

Margaret attended Somerville, which is part of Oxford University. Her tutor, Dorothy Hodgkin, won a Nobel Prize for chemistry in 1964. Margaret studied chemistry but became very interested in politics. She joined the conservative campus politics and worked on the parliament **campaign** for George Worth in 1945. Margaret was hooked on politics by this time! After graduation, she worked in a plastics factory to support herself while she studied law. Margaret felt that studying law would give her a good background for a career in politics.

At the urging of friends, including John Gant, Margaret ran for Parliament but lost the race. She, however, met Denis Thatcher, and they fell in love. Marriage plans were put on hold while she ran for a second time. Voters would not take a married woman seriously. There was still a very strong **double standard** in the way men and women in the professions were viewed. Margaret lost the second race, married in December 1951, and concentrated on becoming a lawyer. She passed the bar exam while expecting the couple's twins.

Margaret ran for Parliament a third time and won. She was elected just before she turned thirty-four. The only downside to any of this was that her father died one day before she was elected. Margaret was appointed parliamentary secretary to the Minister of Pensions and the National Insurance. She was praised for her competence and she always did her homework; she read extensively and knew what she was talking about. She was appointed

Secretary of State for Education and Science and also private advisor to the prime minister. Margaret believed that higher taxes and dependency on government programs worked against quality of life. She once quoted Abraham Lincoln, "You cannot bring prosperity by discouraging thrift." She became leader of the opposition party in 1975 and traveled to the United States, where she met President Ford and Secretary of State Henry Kissinger. Margaret was also interviewed by Barbara Walters. Margaret ran for **prime minister** on the platform to abandon **socialism** because she believed it did not deliver what it promised and that it was actually creating more problems and lowering the standard of living for the British people. She supported a strong stand against communism. A Russian news agency, *TASS*, nicknamed her The Iron Lady. Margaret was a tough politician, standing up for what she believed even when it appeared to be politically unfavorable to do so.

Margaret never forgot people who were alone. On Christmas and other holidays, she gathered up people who had no families and invited them to the family's country home called Chequers (similar to the US presidential retreat, Camp David). She was known for her generous heart.

In June 1982, the Falklands War erupted when a dictator invaded these South Atlantic islands. He tried to force the residents to abdicate their British rights and be swallowed up by his regime based in Argentina. Residents asked for Britain's help. Margaret sent troops to restore peace. The short war ended on June 14, 1982. A year later, in June 1983, she was elected to her second term.

The 1984 bombing of the Grand Hotel that leveled five stories helped persuade Margaret to support President Reagan's attack on terrorist strongholds of Muammar

Qadhafi in Libya. While France was afraid to allow US planes to fly from their bases, Britain was not. Margaret's values and beliefs were very close to those held by Ronald Reagan. They both believed in freedom, democracy, and the free enterprise system. They both viewed the former Soviet Union as the evil empire. Margaret met Mikhail Gorbachev and was impressed with his openness and the move toward allowing Russian people to enjoy more control of their own lives. She and her ally and friend, President Ronald Reagan, encouraged Gorbachev to move his country toward more freedom and a democratic-style government.

Margaret was elected to three terms as Great Britain's prime minister. She served from 1979 to 1990. She held the office for the longest period of any modern prime minister. Margaret decided not to run for a fourth term. In 1993 she entered the House of Lords, one of the two houses of the legislature. With that office came the title Baroness Thatcher of Kesterven. Also in 1993, Margaret's first book, *Volume I: The Downing Years*, was published. It was an autobiography in which she paid tribute to her husband, Denis, who gave her great strength. It was followed by *Volume 2: Statescraft* in 2002 and *Path to Power* published in 1995.

Margaret kept a busy lecture schedule after her retirement from public office until the early 2000s. In December of 2001, Margaret and her husband, Denis, celebrated their golden wedding anniversary in Madeira, Spain, where they had honeymooned fifty years before. Margaret suffered a very mild stroke and had to rest for several days before returning home to England. She had planned five US tours for the summer of 2002 to promote her second book. By March of 2002 Margaret's doctors persuaded her to slow down. On March 23, 2002 Margaret announced that she would make no more public speeches. Her United States tours were cancelled, as well as her plans to attend the June 14, 2002 twentieth anniversary celebration of the end of the Falklands War.

In June of 2004 Margaret attended the memorial service for former US President Ronald Reagan in Washington, DC. She delivered the eulogy by video tape, due to her failing health. She also traveled to California with Reagan's entourage to attend the memorial and burial services at the Reagan Library.

Margaret suffered a final stroke and passed away on April 8, 2013. Her funeral was held at St. Paul's Cathedral and attended by more than two thousand people from her country and from around the world. Representing the United States were former Secretaries of State George Shultz and James A. Baker III, who had both worked with Margaret. Because Margaret had requested no eulogies, Prime Minister David Cameron and Margaret's granddaughter Amanda Thatcher read passages from the King James Bible that they had chosen. Prime Minister Cameron chose the hymns. Margaret's twins, Mark and Carol, placed a note among their mother's coffin flowers that read, "Beloved mother, always in our hearts." After the funeral ceremony, Margaret's remains were cremated and laid to rest in the grounds of the Royal Hospital Chelsea, also the final resting place of her husband, Denis.

Margaret is respected and admired by lovers of freedom and democracy. She will be remembered as a woman of strong moral integrity and a firm belief in democracy. Her husband, Denis, her son, and her daughter were always supportive and proud of her. Margaret has been compared to Winston Churchill for her love of freedom and utmost integrity. She once said,

> We want a society where people are free to make choices, to make mistakes, to be generous and compassionate. This is what we mean by a moral society; not a society where the state is responsible for everything, and no one is responsible for the state.

Margaret always tried to affect positive change by living her life by her father's advice:

> Margaret, never do things just because other people do them. Make up your own mind about what you are going to do, and **persuade** people to go your way.

Margaret learned that in politics as in everyday life, one must stay true to one's own beliefs, even when to do so is unpopular with others. She explained why this is important:

> If you just set out to be liked, you would be prepared to compromise on anything at any time, and you would achieve nothing.

Activity

Ask students to decide what characteristics make a good leader.

(1) Are integrity, honesty, and standing your ground, even when to do so might be politically unwise, still valued?

(2) Should a leader have equal or even higher standards than the average person?

(3) Is there ever a good reason to do the wrong thing?

(4) Encourage the class to share their ideas.

(5) On a blackboard or marker board, list the characteristics students believe a good leader should have.

(6) Who, if there are any leaders today, do students believe have these qualities?

Match vocabulary words with definitions

Use a dictionary to match definitions for the words below, as used in the context of the story.

1. socialism (noun)

2. campaign (noun)

3. double standard (noun)

4. prime minister (noun)

5. persuade (verb)

_____(a) a series of planned actions undertaken to elect a candidate

_____(b) the chief executive of a parliamentary government (similar in duties and power to our president) ____(c) to influence by argument or by asking earnest or urgent questions to bring someone to a belief or course of action

____(d) a set of principles that apply differently and usually more vigorously to one group of people or circumstances than to another

____(e) a form of government advocating collective or governmental ownership and administration of the means of production (in direct opposition to democracy and free enterprise)

Answer questions in complete sentences

1. Why should Margaret Thatcher be remembered?

_____

_____

_____

2. Why do you think Margaret took her education so seriously?

_____

_____

_____

3. Why do you think Margaret decided to run for prime minister?

_____

_____

_____

4. Margaret said that her father was the biggest influence in her life. Who has been most influential in your life? How has that person helped you?

_____

_____

_____

Harriet Tubman:
They Called Her Moses

HARRIET TUBMAN WAS born in 1815. She was one of eleven children born to Ben Ross and Harriet Green, enslaved workers on the plantation of Edward Brodas on the eastern shore of Chesapeake Bay in Maryland. Like many slaves, Harriet was forced to work when she was very little and even when she was ill.

Harriet's family was not allowed to attend church or school. However, they met whenever possible with other enslaved people to share stories and news from other plantations. Harriet grew up hearing stories about uprisings—slaves fighting back. She loved the stories in the Bible. Her favorite was Moses because he led his people out of slavery. Many enslaved people pretended to be content to please their slave owners. Harriet, however, refused to pretend to be happy to **appease** her slave owner. Even as a child, she had pride in who she was!

When she had the measles, Harriet was a **scrawny** child and very ill, yet she was made to work anyway. The weak little child nearly died. She was only about four or five years old yet was expected to take care of a white infant. When Harriet could not keep the baby from crying or did anything that displeased her masters, she was beaten. She was often farmed out to neighbors. Once, Harriet was expected to learn weaving so that she could do the weaving back on her owner's plantation. Plantations were more than homes. Because they were mostly in rural areas, they needed to be as self-sufficient as possible. In addition to growing food, they also produced the raw fibers, such as cotton and wool used in making fabric for clothing. The enslaved people did all the work, often specializing in field work with crops or animals or working in the big house cooking, cleaning, weaving, sewing, and laundering. Even tiny slave children were made to be productive.

At age ten Harriet was put out in the fields to do heavy labor. By this time there were harsher laws to prevent slaves from gaining any power through association with others. Slaves were not allowed to gather in groups or talk while working. The very bloody Nat Turner revolt in 1831 scared slave owners. Many were fearful that their slaves would revolt if given any chance to organize themselves.

In an unfortunate accident, Harriet suffered a bad head injury when a storeowner threw a heavy metal object. It had been intended for another slave who was running away, but it missed and hit Harriet in the head. After that Harriet often collapsed into unconsciousness with no warning. In time she learned to use it to her advantage, pretending to be weak and **disoriented** even when she was not. Whenever Harriet's owner tried to sell her, she faked fainting spells and weakness. Her family supported her pretense so that she would not be separated from them. Slaves who were weak or sickly were not easy to sell. It was a common practice to sell members of a slave family to other owners. Many children and parents were separated and sold to new owners, even out of state.

When Harriet was a young woman, she married a free black man named John Tubman. Their marriage did not last long, but Harriet kept John's last name. News spread that her slave owner Brodas was going to sell many of his slaves. It was clearly time to escape. Harriet turned to a white neighbor who had offered to help. Harriet escaped by going from safe home to safe home until she reached Pennsylvania. The northern states had already outlawed slavery, so slaves headed north to the free states. Harriet said,

> When I found I had crossed the line, I looked at my hands to see if I was the same person. There was such a glory over everything. The sun came like gold through the trees, and over the fields, and I felt like I was in heaven!

Within the next few years, Harriet brought her parents, brothers, sisters, friends, and others north to freedom. In all, she was responsible for helping over three hundred men, women, and children to escape to freedom.

There was a $40,000.00 reward for the capture of the slave **liberator**. This was a great deal of money in the mid-1800s. Harriet became known as Moses because, like her favorite biblical person, she led her people to freedom. Most slave owners thought this liberator was a man. They never imagined that a small woman could accomplish what Harriet was doing! Railroads were the latest mode of transportation in the mid-nineteenth century. When Harriet first escaped, she seemed to have just disappeared. Someone remarked that she must have ridden away on an invisible railroad. This quickly developed into the **underground railroad**. Harriet was the most famous "conductor" of the system—a series of safe houses throughout the South where people hid and fed slaves on their secret journey northward to freedom. Not everyone in the South supported the institution of slavery.

Only one in four Southerners owned even one slave. But the laws protected the slave owners. Those people who assisted slaves did so at great risk to themselves. During the Civil War, Harriet worked as a nurse, a scout, and as a spy for the North.

After the war, Harriet made her home in Auburn, New York. She fought for women's right to vote, helped create schools for black students, and helped the poor, old, and helpless in many ways. Harriet was a Christian who did not take her blessings for granted. Her door was always open to people in need. Harriet died on March 10, 1913 at the age of ninety-eight. The lady called Moses was honored with a military funeral.

Activity

Harriet Tubman was the most famous of the underground railroad conductors. As part of a large network of abolitionists throughout the southern, eastern, and midwestern United States, she and others helped slaves gain their freedom. Assisting enslaved people could be a very dangerous undertaking until slavery was made illegal by the Thirteenth Amendment. Below are a list of some abolitionists and where they lived/worked to support freedom.

1. John Brown, MA

2. Rufus Elmer, MA

3. Rev. Dr. Samuel Osgood, MA

4. Thomas Thomas, MA

5. Dr. George White, MA

6. Dr. Jefferson Church, MA

7. Reuben Atwater Chapman, MA

8. Henry Bibb and wife, Mary Bibb, Ontario, Canada

9. William and Francis Jackson, MA

10. Rev. John Milton Holmes, NJ

11. Arthur and Lewis Tappan, MA

12. Stephen Myers, NY

13. William Still, PA

14. Robert Purvis, PA

15. Susan B. Anthony, NY

16. Abigail Goodwin, NJ

17. Harriet Jacobs, NY
18. Jonathan Walker, FL
19. Fredrick Douglass, Washington, DC
20. Louisa May Alcott, MA
21. John Everett, NJ
22. David Le Holder, NJ

Useful websites:

www.eiu.edu/eiutp/UndergroundRailroad ResourceBooklet.pdf
www.scholastic.com/teachers/lesson-plan/ path-freedom

Directions for Activity

(1) Each student will choose from the list above or find another abolitionist to research. Students may work individually or as a small group.

(2) Students will gather information and write one-page reports that include abolitionist's:

(a) upbringing and early history

(b) religious and/or philosophical views, if any

(c) profession (some were physicians, ministers, shopkeepers, authors, journalists, newspaper editors, ship captains, etc.)

(d) their contributions to freedom for enslaved people

Match vocabulary words with definitions

Use a dictionary to match definitions for the words below, as used in the context of the story.

1. appease (verb)

2. scrawny (adjective)

3. disoriented (verb)

4. liberator (noun)

5. underground railroad (noun)

____(a) extremely lean, skinny, or puny

____(b) a person who frees others from bondage

____(c) a system of cooperation and safe houses among active antislavery people who before and during the American Civil War helped enslaved people reach freedom in the North

____(d) confused; cause to lose bearings or sense of location or identity

____(e) pacify, calm, or cause to subside

Answer questions in complete sentences

1. Why should Harriet Tubman be remembered?

_____

_____

_____

2. How did Harriet use an injury to benefit herself?

_____

_____

_____

3. How did Harriet help so many slaves escape to freedom?

_____

_____

_____

4. What evidence is there that Harriet was thankful for her blessings?

_____

_____

_____

Edith Wilson: The Presidentress

EDITH BOLING GALT Wilson was born the seventh of eleven children on October 15, 1872 in Wytheville, Virginia. She was a direct descendent of Pocahontas on her father's side of the family. While growing up, Edith spent many happy afternoons with her paternal Grandmother Boling who lived with the family. Edith learned much from this elderly lady who acted as her informal teacher.

Edith later attended a private girls' boarding school in Abindon, Virginia, where she grew to love music. Edith's education was cut short so that her younger brothers could be educated. Family finances were tight, and in the late nineteenth and early twentieth centuries, a boy's education was deemed essential while a girl's education was viewed as somewhat of an **extravagance**. It was normal for families to make sacrifices to educate sons but not to educate daughters. Edith accepted this but continued to read everything she could to help satisfy her ambition and interests in education.

As a young woman Edith traveled to Washington, DC, to live with her married sister. Edith enjoyed the activity of a busy city. There she met Norman Galt, and they soon fell in love and were married in 1908. The couple was very happy together and thrilled with the birth of a son. Their joy turned to despair when the infant died after three days. Their sorrow was intensified when they learned that they would be unable to have any more children. After

Norman also died, Edith busied herself in the running of the Galt family jewelry store. She proved herself to be a very quick learner and a most competent businesswoman. With both her husband and father deceased, Edith was the sole support for her mother, unmarried sister, and younger brothers. Edith never complained but threw her energies into the business.

Edith's friend, Altrude Gordon, dated the White House physician Dr. Cary Grayson, who had treated Ellen Wilson, wife of the president, before she died. Dr. Grayson was concerned about Helen Bones, the sad cousin of the president, who was grieving for her friend Ellen. He asked Edith to become Helen's friend because they had so much in common. While visiting Helen, Edith bumped into the president on several occasions before he asked her to go for an afternoon automobile ride with him in Washington, DC. In those days it was safe for the president to enjoy excursions without being always surrounded by Secret Service bodyguards. The couple became friends and soon after realized they loved each other. Wilson was the widowed father of three grown daughters, who were relieved that their father had someone special with whom to share his life. They married in a quiet ceremony in the White House with only family and close friends present. Edith was forty-two, and Woodrow was fifty-eight years old. The age difference was never an issue because their interests made them so **compatible**.

Edith dearly loved orchids. They were by far her favorite flowers. Woodrow delighted in sending her one each day. He once remarked, "You are the only woman who I know who can wear an orchid. On everybody else the orchid wears the woman."

Edith supported her husband in everything he did. He won reelection in 1916; however, Edith did not vote for him. She did not vote for anyone. She could not. Women were not allowed to vote until four years later in 1920 when they finally won the right with the addition of the Nineteenth Amendment to the United States Constitution. Strangely, Edith's husband and the Democrats did not support women's suffrage. It was the Republican Party that stood with the women in their quest for the right to vote. Eventually, President Wilson parted with his political party on the issue and supported the Nineteenth Amendment after it became politically expedient to do so.

Edith helped with the war effort at home during World War I. She placed sheep on the White House lawn to graze, thus freeing the gardeners to do work that helped support the US in World War I. Those sheep produced ninety-eight pounds of wool that earned $100,000.00 at a benefit auction for the Red Cross! That was a substantial amount of money a hundred years ago. Edith was her husband's most trusted advisor. She was one of only a few trusted people who were **privy** to national secrets. Edith was also very **astute** at decoding secret codes that had been intercepted from the enemies of the US and its allies.

After WWI the couple traveled to Europe to promote the League of Nations, an early predecessor of the United Nations. Woodrow also worked on the terms of the peace treaty. Edith and Woodrow were the first presidential couple to travel outside the United States during their White House years. This caused some criticism from people who believed that a president "should stay home." After all, no president had done this before. The Wilsons won the hearts of the French people. Everywhere Edith ventured, people gave her flowers and came out just to see her. The Versailles Treaty was signed and supported by Europeans, but many Americans did not trust it. They thought that it did not have the best interests of America at heart. The Wilsons were very disappointed.

Upon returning home, the couple set out on a harried cross-country trip. The purpose of the journey was to convince the American people that the League of Nations would ensure world cooperation and peace and also help prevent war. World War I had been called "the war to end all wars." Woodrow functioned at a near-exhausted pace much of the time. On the way home, he suffered a stroke. Edith took over the day-to-day activities of the president, only consulting him on affairs that she deemed absolutely necessary. Above all else she wanted to help him recover. Dr. Grayson thought the president should resign, but Edith feared that resigning would erode his will to live. The two of them protected him around the clock. They screened all visitors and only told the president about matters that required his personal input. Some people criticized Edith's strength and called her the Iron Queen, the Presidentress, and America's First Woman President. In Edith's autobiography, *My Memoir*, she defended herself saying, "The only decision that was mine was what was important and what was not, and the very important decision of when to present matters to my husband."

America never ratified the League of Nations that was created in Geneva in 1920. This was a grave disappointment to Woodrow. President Wilson, however, was awarded the Nobel Peace Prize.

After Woodrow's second presidential term was completed, the couple retired. Once again they enjoyed afternoon drives in their car and Saturday movies. Woodrow made a radio speech on Veterans Day in 1923. A careful listener could hear Edith in the background prompting her husband because he was still weak from the stroke. Woodrow died in 1924. At the time of his death, he was writing a book. It was never completed. In fact, Woodrow never got beyond the dedication to his wife, Edith.

Edith continued to be respected and loved by a grateful nation. Eleanor and Franklin Roosevelt often invited her to White House social events. She was even in the gallery of Congress with Eleanor when Franklin asked Congress to declare war on Japan during World War II. That occasion reminded Edith of the time her own husband had asked Congress to declare war on Germany during World War I in 1917. In 1945 the United Nations' opening ceremony paid tribute to Woodrow Wilson. This was a proud moment for his **widow**. Over the years Edith remained active in national events. She supported the campaign of John F. Kennedy in 1960 and rode in his inaugural parade. She died on December 28, 1961 at the age of eighty-nine. This was exactly 105 years after the birth of her beloved husband, Woodrow.

Activity

Edith loved orchids and often wore one singly as a corsage. Orchids come in a variety of shapes and sizes, as well as in an array of colors such as white, yellow, green, lavender, purple, and burgundy.

Students will enjoy creating an orchid with crepe paper and pipe cleaners.

For each orchid:

(1) Cut three ovals of crepe paper about five by two inches each for the petals. Trim both ends of the ovals into slanted points.

(2) At the center of each petal, cut small notches on either side.

(3) Place three petals at angles on top one another so that there are three points above and three points below, equidistance from each other.

(4) Twist a pipe cleaner in its center to make a small half-inch loop. Poke two tiny holes 1/4 inch apart in the center of the petals. Push both ends of pipe cleaner through holes until the small loop is all showing atop the petals.

(5) Twist one side of pipe cleaner around the base of the flower, pulling petals together to resemble an orchid. Bend the other pipe cleaner half into a small figure eight scrunched up behind the blossom.

(6) Push a corsage pin through the pipe cleaner in a figure eight on the back of the orchid to attach to clothing. Corsage pins are often available at craft stores.

Match vocabulary words with definitions

Use a dictionary to match definitions for the words below, as used in the context of the biography.

1. extravagance (noun)
2. compatible (adjective)
3. privy (adjective)
4. astute (adjective)
5. widow (noun)

____(a) clever, ingenious, or keenly discerning

____(b) personal, secret, private; admitted as one sharing in a secret

____(c) wasteful, costly, or unwise expense

____(d) able to exist or act together harmoniously

____(e) a woman who has lost her husband by death and has not remarried

Answer questions in complete sentences

1. Why should Edith Wilson be remembered?

_____

_____

_____

2. Why was Edith's formal education cut short?

_____

_____

_____

3. How did Edith meet Woodrow Wilson?

_____

_____

_____

4. How did Edith help her country during World War I?

_____

_____

_____

Answer Keys

Abigail Adams

Match vocabulary words with definitions

1. correspondence
2. establish
3. garrets
4. escapade
5. conferring

> 5 (a) discussing and consulting something together; comparing opinions and ideas

> 3 (b) attics, usually small, cramped ones

> 1 (c) communication by exchanging letters

> 2 (d) to bring into being on a firm or permanent basis; found

> 4 (e) a reckless adventure or wild prank, especially one that is contrary to usual or proper behavior

Answer questions in complete sentences

1. <u>Why should Abigail Adams be remembered?</u>

   Abigail was studious and engaged in national interests during most of her life. She raised her children with sound values, mostly by herself, as she supported her husband's government work. Abigail worked their farm and saved enough money to guarantee a comfortable retirement for John and herself. She supported abolition of slavery and women's rights.

2. How did Rover accidently save the gunpowder in the church garret?

Rover growled and scratched at the garret door because he wanted out. The boys thought those sounds were made by ghosts and the devil. Terrified, they abandoned their plan to steal gunpowder.

3. Why did Abigail and John find a soul mate in each other?

Both Abigail and John were well-read and intelligent, interested in government and politics, loved to discuss their opinions, plus they deeply loved each other.

4. Besides reading a biography about Abigail, how could we learn more about her adult life?

We could read the two volumes of letters exchanged between Abigail and John during their times apart. These volumes were published by their grandson, Charles Francis Adams, in 1876.

Louisa May Alcott

Match vocabulary words with definitions

1. progressive
2. adhered
3. deficient
4. solitude
5. sacrificed

   5 (a) accepted the loss or destruction of something desirable for a higher cause, end, or ideal

   1 (b) advancing, making continuous improvement toward better conditions, open-minded ideas, and more enlightenment

   4 (c) seclusion, the state of being alone

   2 (d) devoted to or followed closely

   3 (e) inadequate, lacking some element or consideration

Answer questions in complete sentences

1. Why should Louisa May Alcott be remembered?

   Louisa became a professional writer whose many books have been enjoyed by generations of readers. She financially supported her family. Louisa raised her deceased sister's daughter as her own. Louisa purchased a home for her mother and cared for her ailing father until his death.

2. In following the Grahamism diet, what foods were consumed? What foods were avoided?

Fruits, vegetables, whole grains, chicken, fish, milk, and water were consumed. Red meat, refined sugar, and alcohol were avoided.

3. <u>What did Louisa sacrifice to become a professional writer?</u>

   She sacrificed marriage and motherhood.

4. <u>Name at least two reasons why Louisa became a professional writer.</u>

   Louisa enjoyed reading, writing, and creating stories. She wanted to financially support her family, knowing that writing paid well because Harriet Beecher Stowe had earned her living as an author.

Marian Anderson

Match vocabulary words with definitions

1. modest

2. congregation

3. prodigy

4. spiritual

5. prejudice

   2 (a) an assembly of people brought together for common religious worship

   3 (b) a person, especially a child or young person, having an extraordinary talent or ability

   5 (c) an opinion for or against something or someone without adequate basis

1 (d) free from showy extravagance; simple, small, or plain

4 (e) religious song, especially originating among enslaved African Americans in the southern United States

Answer questions in complete sentences

1. Why should Marian Anderson be remembered?

    Marian had a natural, God-given talent for singing that she worked hard to develop. She reached multicultural audiences. Marian was a role model for black singers who came after her. She donated money for student scholarships, usually anonymously. Marian supported herself and her widowed mother. She never allowed fame or money to change her Christian values.

2. Name two kinds of songs that Marian sang at her concerts.

    Marian sang spirituals, operas, and sometimes European songs in native European languages.

3. Name two instruments that Marian learned to play as a child.

    Marian learned to play the piano as well as the violin.

4. Name some of the people who supported Marian's interest and career in music and explain how they helped her.

1. Her parents bought Marian a piano. Her mother taught Marian not to take her talent for granted.

2. Her church made her a choir member as a child.

3. Marian's high school principal encouraged her to attend a school with a better music program.

4. Another principal took Marian to a special music teacher.

5. Giuseppe Boghetti gave her private lessons.

6. Her church collected money for lessons.

7. Roland Hayes arranged for singing opportunities.

8. Mary Sanders gave Marian private lessons.

9. The Philadelphia Choral Society gave Marian a scholarship.

10. Jean Sibelius, Arturo Toscanini, and Kosti Vehanen encouraged and helped Marian with concert tours.

11. Eleanor Roosevelt arranged for Marian to sing before the Lincoln Memorial in 1939 because of her talent and also to further civil rights.

12. The US government made Marian an alternate delegate to the United Nations and asked her to tour Asia in 1951.

Elizabeth Blackwell

Match vocabulary words with definitions

1. potential
2. convictions
3. midwife

4. infirmary

5. affiliated

5 (a) associated closely with

3 (b) a woman who assists women in childbirth

1 (c) possibility, an ability that may or may not be developed or realized

4 (d) a hospital; a place for the care of the sick or injured

2 (e) fixed or firm beliefs

Answer questions in complete sentences

1. <u>Why should Elizabeth Blackwell be remembered?</u>

Elizabeth worked hard to become a doctor and was the first female American doctor. She trained nurses during the Civil War. She founded a teaching hospital to help patients and to train other women who wanted to become doctors. Elizabeth helped decrease death rates for new mothers and babies with hygiene changes. She gave talks and wrote medical books. She founded the National Health Society of London and was the head of gynecology and a professor at London School of Medicine.

2. <u>Why did it take Elizabeth so long to become a doctor?</u>

Elizabeth had to earn a living and save money for college. All but one American medical school refused to admit her. Most people believed the prejudice that women should become nurses, not doctors.

3. <u>What prevented Elizabeth from becoming a surgeon?</u>

Elizabeth accidentally splashed some strong medicine in one eye, blinding that eye. A surgeon cannot have limited vision.

4. <u>What did Elizabeth do to help other women become doctors?</u>

Elizabeth founded a hospital and medical school for women (the New York Infirmary for Women and Children), founded the National Health Society of London, and was a professor and head of gynecology at the London School of Medicine.

Nellie Bly

Match vocabulary words with definitions

1. articulate

2. rebuttal

3. pen name

4. perils

5. benefactor

1 (a) clear, distinct, and precise

2 (b) the act of providing some evidence or argument that refutes or opposes

4 (c) dangers, risks, jeopardy

5 (d) a person who gives help, especially of a financial nature

3 (e) a name used by a writer other than their own

Answer questions in complete sentences

1. Why should Nellie Bly (Elizabeth Cochrane) be remembered?

   Nellie supported herself and her family by becoming a successful journalist. She led the way for investigative reporters. She exposed and addressed social problems. Nellie was a war correspondent during World War I. She helped destitute women find jobs to support themselves and their children. Nellie helped orphaned and abandoned children find loving, permanent families.

2. Why would Nellie Bly's true identity have been an embarrassment for her family when she was a reporter for the *Pittsburgh Dispatch*?

   If Nellie's identity had been known, the whole community would know that her dead father had not provided for his family and that the family was financially dependent on a seventeen-year-old female.

3. What noteworthy undertaking caused Nellie Bly to become world famous?

   Nellie traveled around the world in a much-publicized trip while racing the clock and beating the record of Jules Verne's fictional character, Phineas Fogg.

4. To what causes did Nellie Bly devote much of her time and energies during the last years of her life?

Nellie wrote an advice column for women and helped many destitute women find jobs to support themselves and their children. She also helped abandoned and orphaned children find permanent families, taking in one child herself.

Barbara Bush

Match vocabulary words with definitions

1. excelled

2. devastating

3. credentials

4. avid

5. literacy

    3 (a) evidence of authority, status, rights, or credit

    4 (b) enthusiastic, eager, or dedicated

    5 (c) ability to read and write competently

    1 (d) surpassed or been superior in some respect

    2 (e) emotionally overwhelming, greatly troubling

Answer questions in complete sentences

1. <u>Why should Barbara Bush be remembered?</u>

    Barbara is a positive role model. She raised a happy, successful family. She supported her husband in all his pursuits. Barbara donated profits from her books to charity. She continues to work for charities, including the Barbara Bush Foundation for Family Literacy. She has enjoyed a long and loving marriage with her husband. Barbara is only the second woman to be the wife of a president and the mother of a president. She is much admired and respected for her good works.

2. <u>What aspects of being a politician's wife has Barbara especially enjoyed?</u>

   Barbara has enjoyed traveling and living in many different places, especially in the White House and China.

3. <u>While First Lady, what did Barbara do to help promote literacy?</u>

   Barbara wrote a book with her dog, Millie, and donated the profits to charity. She set up The Barbara Bush Foundation for Family Literacy.

4. <u>According to Barbara, at the end of one's life, what might a person regret instead of lost career opportunities?</u>

   A person might regret having not spent more time with family and friends.

Marie Curie

Match vocabulary words with definitions

1. heritage
2. typhus
3. elements
4. generosity
5. dedicated

4 (a) unselfishness, willingness and eagerness to share with others

1 (b) traditions handed down from one's ancestors

3 (c) basic substances that cannot be separated into simpler substances

2 (d) a serious and potentially fatal disease characterized by reddish spots on the skin, severe headache, sustained high fever, and extreme weakness or exhaustion

5 (e) wholly committed or devoted to something such as a cause, goal, or purpose

Answer questions in complete sentences

1. <u>Why should Marie Curie be remembered?</u>

Marie and her sister took turns working to pay for each other's college educations. She discovered two new elements, radium and polonium. Marie was the first woman to win a Nobel Prize and the first person to win a second Nobel Prize. She used her money and fame to further research in X-ray technology and cancer treatments. She saved many lives during World War I with the portable X-ray units set up for wounded soldiers. Marie did not let grief or adversity stop her from reaching her goals. She wanted to be remembered as a good mother and a good scientist.

2. <u>What evidence showed that Marie was intellectually gifted at a young age?</u>

Marie learned her alphabet and started putting words together when she was four. She had an excellent memory. Marie was an avid reader and read everything she could find. She explored the microscope and jars in her father's study. Marie learned several foreign languages. She could concentrate even when much activity and distractions surrounded her.

3. What obstacles did Marie face and overcome in achieving a college education?

   Females were not allowed to attend college in Poland, so Marie worked and saved money to attend college in France. She studied and learned in the secret Floating University, even at the risk of being arrested.

4. What evidence shows that Marie remained hardworking and modest throughout her entire professional life?

   Marie was one of the most famous women in the world, yet she used her money and fame to further research and to help people. Her daughters and her work were more important to her than fame. Marie wanted to be remembered as a good mother and a good scientist.

Jan Davis

Match vocabulary words with definitions

1. biographies
2. mechanical engineering
3. astronaut

4. simulators

5. payload commander

3 (a) highly trained pilot who holds multiple degrees in various sciences and travels in outer space

2 (b) a branch of engineering making practical use of pure sciences dealing with the design and production of machinery

4 (c) laboratory devices used for the purpose of training or experimentation that enable the operator to reproduce under test conditions phenomena likely to occur in actual performance

5 (d) the person in charge of the cargo transported on a space shuttle such as satellites or medical or scientific experiments

1 (e) written histories of persons' lives

Answer questions in complete sentences

1. Why should Jan Davis be remembered?

Jan is a highly trained space shuttle astronaut. She was the payload commander on one flight and piloted the shuttle. Jan worked on many important engineering projects to improve the space program.

2. What kinds of books did Jan like to read when she was a child?

Jan liked to read biographies and *Nancy Drew* mysteries.

3. Why did Jan not consider a career as an astronaut earlier in life?

When Jan was a child and a young woman, all astronauts were men. Becoming an astronaut did not seem to be a career open to women.

4. What advice did Jan offer about achieving your goals?

Jan said, "Select a field you will enjoy studying, do your best, and if you do not achieve your goal the first time, keep trying."

Amelia Earhart

Match vocabulary words with definitions

1. foreshadowed

2. soloed

3. monsoons

4. reconnaissance

5. aviator

2 (a) flew an airplane alone without a companion or partner

1 (b) showed or indicated beforehand

5 (c) a pilot of an airplane or other heavier-than-air aircraft

3 (d) seasonal winds in the Indian and Pacific Oceans that usually bring heavy rains to southern and western areas of Asia

4 (e) exploratory military survey of enemy territory

Answer questions in complete sentences

1. <u>Why should Amelia Earhart be remembered?</u>

   Amelia was one of the first female pilots. She set many speed and distance records in flight. She was the first woman to cross the Atlantic by airplane and the first woman to solo the Atlantic Ocean from North America to Europe. Amelia attempted to circumnavigate the world near the Equator by airplane and completed most of the distance. She wrote books about her flying experiences and encouraged children to work toward their goals.

2. <u>How was Amelia's childhood different from that of most other girls during the early years of the twentieth century?</u>

   Amelia's parents encouraged her to explore her interests and not allow gender to restrict her goals. They gave Amelia toys she requested, that were viewed by many others as only appropriate for boys.

3. <u>If Amelia had survived her round-the-world flight, what do you think she would have done with the rest of her life? Why?</u>

   Answers will vary.

4. <u>If Amelia had lived in our time, what do you think she would be doing today? Why?</u>

   Answers will vary.

Ruth Heller

Match vocabulary words with definitions

1. immigration
2. ideal
3. freelance
4. aesthetically
5. inspired

5 (a) influenced, moved, or guided emotionally or intellectually

4 (b) beautifully appealing to the mind and emotions

3 (c) independent, working, or pursuing a profession without a long-term contract or commitment to any employer

2 (d) regarded as perfect in its category, excellent, or highly desirable

1 (e) movement into a country of which one is not a native and taking up permanent residence

Answer questions in complete sentences

1. Why should Ruth Heller be remembered?

Ruth has written and illustrated many educational and beautiful books.

2. Why did Ruth live in several different communities as a child?

Ruth's father wanted his family to live in the best place in the world. He thought San Francisco was the ideal place to raise a family. They moved from Manitoba to Vancouver, British Columbia, while they were waiting to migrate to San Francisco.

3. <u>What were Ruth's first paid jobs as a professional artist?</u>

Ruth's first jobs were designing gift-wrap, other paper products, newspaper advertisements, posters, puzzles, and coloring books.

4. <u>How is Ruth's childhood reflected in her artwork?</u>

Ruth included royal characters in some of her books because she had lived in a neighborhood where the streets were named for kings and queens. She featured seashell and sea creatures because she fondly remembered the beautiful beaches that border Vancouver. Ruth drew butterflies from memories of a willow tree filled with caterpillars she had collected and kept until they turned into lovely butterflies.

Mahalia Jackson

Match vocabulary words with definitions

1. debut
2. castoffs
3. volunteer
4. proceeds
5. gospel music

    4 (a) the profits or returns from a sale or other business transaction

3 (b) a person who offers his or her services for some purpose or undertaking without charging a fee

5 (c) music that deals with the life of Jesus Christ and his teachings

1 (d) the first public appearance on stage

2 (e) garments discarded or rejected

Answer questions in complete sentences

1. <u>Why should Mahalia Jackson be remembered?</u>

Mahalia worked hard all her life. She was a talented gospel singer. Mahalia was generous with her talent and money. She introduced black gospel music to worldwide multicultural audiences. Mahalia donated to charities and student scholarships.

2. <u>Describe some of the difficulties Mahalia faced as a child.</u>

Mahalia's family was very poor. She helped grow vegetables, as well as catch fish, shellfish, and alligators for food. She worked dressing wealthy children before school. Mahalia lived with an aunt and uncle and only saw her beloved father on weekends after her mother died. Mahalia quit school after eighth grade to work. Later, she put aside her plans for attending nursing school to support herself and her sick aunt.

3. <u>Why did Mahalia decline offers to sing with many famous black entertainers and bands?</u>

Mahalia said the blues were too sad, and she preferred to sing songs of hope and faith.

4. Describe some of the ways Mahalia was generous
   with her talent and money.

   Mahalia sang at civil rights events. She donated
   concert proceeds to charities. Mahalia established
   scholarships for poor, but academically talented
   students of various races. She wrote a book and
   a cookbook to share what she had learned in life.
   Mahalia toured and entertained our troops abroad,
   even after her doctors warned her to slow down for
   her health.

Princess Kaiulani

Match vocabulary words with definitions

1. christened

2. banyan

3. haoles

4. abdicate

5. annexation

   5 (a) the act of adding something, especially territory

   4 (b) to formally give up or relinquish one's throne

   2 (c) an East Indian fig tree whose branches send
   out roots to the ground, sometimes causing
   the tree to spread over a wide area

   1 (d) to give a child a name at the time of Christian
   baptism

   3 (e) non-Polynesians, non-native Hawaiians

Answer questions in complete sentences

1. <u>Why should Princess Kaiulani be remembered?</u>

   Kaiulani was the last Hawaiian of royal birth. She would have been queen and she prepared for those duties. Kaiulani tried to help her people by appealing to the US president to prevent the hostile overthrow of her aunt, the queen. Kauilani was kind and unspoiled her entire life.

2. <u>What did the dying Princess Miriam predict about her daughter's future that came true?</u>

   Miriam said that her daughter would travel far from home, be gone a long time, and that she would never marry or become queen.

3. <u>How did Kaiulani prepare for her future as Hawaii's next queen?</u>

   Kaiulani traveled to England to study at a special girls school. She appealed to President Cleveland to prevent the haoles from overthrowing the royal throne. She put the well-being of her fellow Hawaiians above her own.

4. <u>Why was the end of the young princess' short life so sad?</u>

   Her aunt, the queen, had been arrested and sentenced to hard labor. The spirit of the Hawaiians was broken like Kaiulani's own heart. She became very ill and was in and out of consciousness for weeks before she died.

Juliette Gordon Low

Match vocabulary words with definitions

1. determined
2. scarlet fever
3. apprehensive
4. channel
5. goodwill

   4 (a) to direct toward or through some particular course

   3 (b) anxious, uneasy, fearful

   5 (c) benevolence; cheerful or friendly disposition

   2 (d) a contagious disease caused by streptococcus and characterized by red eruptions on the skin

   1 (e) resolute, unwaveringly decided, staunch

Answer questions in complete sentences

1. <u>Why should Juliette Gordon Low be remembered?</u>

   Juliette founded the Girl Scouts of America. She set up "World Camps" to promote goodwill and peace. Juliette volunteered to nurse wounded soldiers and secured milk and food for them during the Spanish-American War.

2. <u>How did the Civil War change young Juliette's life?</u>

   Juliette's father was a Confederate soldier who moved Juliette, her mother, and sister to Chicago to live safely with relatives during the war. She had little time with her father during that period but became better acquainted with relatives in Chicago. Juliette learned about her great-grandmother who had been determined like Juliette. Juliette was nicknamed Daisy while in Chicago, and that name was designated many years later in Girls Scouts for a certain age group.

3. <u>How did Juliette lose most of her hearing?</u>

Juliette lost most of the hearing in one ear from an experimental silver nitrate treatment she insisted her doctor use for an infection. She lost the hearing in the other ear from a severe infection caused by a grain of rice embedded in her ear that had been thrown at her wedding.

4. <u>What kind of skills did Girl Scouts learn in the early days of scouting?</u>

Girl Scouts learned survival skills such as tracking, exploring, first aid, map reading, signaling, knot tying, and cooking.

Wilma Mankiller

Match vocabulary words with definitions

1. drought
2. descent
3. wake-up call
4. exodus
5. chief

5 (a) the head or leader of an organization

1 (b) a period of dry weather without any rain especially injurious to crops

4 (c) a departure or emigration usually of a large number of people

3 (d) a catalyst or something that alerts or makes a situation apparently clear to someone, especially a situation that necessitates action to remedy

2 (e) lineage, derivation from an ancestor

Answer questions in complete sentences

1. <u>Why should Wilma Mankiller be remembered?</u>

   Wilma worked to improve the lives of Cherokee people. She helped her people become more self-sufficient by teaching them how to repair their homes and install water systems. Wilma became deputy chief and then chief of the Cherokee Nation. She received much recognition and many awards for her good works.

2. <u>What events in Wilma's childhood greatly changed her family's life?</u>

   A two-year drought destroyed the strawberry crops that were her family's source of income. At about the same time, the federal government moved Indians to cities in the belief that urban areas provided more opportunities for jobs and housing.

3. <u>When the Cherokee had been moved from their ancestral lands to Oklahoma, what steps did they take to improve their lives?</u>

They drew up a constitution, built roads and schools, and settled onto farms and ranches creating a thriving community.

4. <u>How did Wilma become chief of the Cherokee?</u>

Wilma had much experience as tribal planner, program director, and deputy chief. When her boss became director of the Bureau of Indian Affairs, Wilma was the best choice for chief and was elected.

Sandra Day O'Connor

Match vocabulary words with definitions

1. attorney

2. bar exam

3. integrity

4. ambiguous

5. unanimously

5 (a) completely in agreement

1 (b) a legal agent qualified to act for persons in legal proceedings

3 (c) honesty, uprightness, soundness of and adherence to moral principles and character

4 (d) having several possible meanings or interpretations; not clear

2 (e) tests one must pass to be licensed as an attorney

Answer questions in complete sentences

1. <u>Why should Sandra Day O'Connor be remembered?</u>

   Sandra was the first woman Supreme Court Justice. She did much volunteer work and helped write questions for the Arizona Bar Exam while she raised her young sons. Sandra was assistant attorney general of Arizona. She was a state senator and Arizona State majority leader. Sandra always did her homework in court cases and made decisions very carefully.

2. <u>How did Sandra's parents encourage her to achieve her potential?</u>

   They gave Sandra the same responsibilities and chores around the ranch that they would have given her had she been a boy. They kept reading materials in their home. They encouraged Sandra's interests. They sent her to live with grandparents in Texas so Sandra could attend school. They sent her to Stanford University.

3. <u>What effect did Professor Rathbun's statement have on Sandra's education and career choice?</u>

   Sandra realized that one person could make positive changes in the world. She thought studying law offered her more opportunities to do so than studying business, which had been her intended major in college.

4. <u>How did Sandra successfully combine family life and a career?</u>

Sandra quit work and stayed home with her children while they were little. She used her free time to do volunteer legal work. She worked part-time when she returned to work. Sandra's State Senate jobs were part-time positions. She and her husband were always involved in all aspects of their sons' lives.

Rosa Parks

Match vocabulary words with definitions

1. discriminated

2. segregated

3. arrested

4. boycott

5. empower

2 (a) separated or set apart from others because of race, religion, etc., often by force

3 (b) seized a person by legal authority or warrant; taken into custody

5 (c) to enable or permit, give power or authority

1 (d) made a distinction in favor of or against a person or thing on the basis of the group, class, or category to which the person or thing belongs, rather than according to actual merit

4 (e) the practice of abstaining from or preventing dealings with by means of intimidation or coercion

Answer questions in complete sentences

1. Why should Rosa Parks be remembered?

   By refusing to surrender her bus seat, Rosa provided the reason for the Montgomery Bus Boycott, which ended in the Supreme Court ruling segregations as being unconstitutional. Rosa worked for civil rights most of her adult life. She established the Rosa and Raymond Parks Institute of Self-Development.

2. How was Rosa's childhood different from the childhoods of white children her age?

   Because Rosa was black, she was discriminated against and segregated in many aspects of life such as schools, restrooms, restaurants, shops, theaters, buses, etc., unlike white children.

3. Why do you think Rosa has become known as the Mother of the Civil Rights Movement?

   By refusing to surrender her bus seat, Rosa provided the stimulus for the boycott that led to the law being changed. This provided nationwide attention to civil rights.

4. What did Rosa do to help others achieve their goals, after her husband, Sylvester, died?

   Rosa founded the Raymond and Rosa Parks Institute of Self-Development to help others complete their educations.

Eleanor Roosevelt

Match vocabulary words with definitions

1. trauma

2. alcoholism

3. diphtheria

4. excursions

5. intervened

   4 (a) brief pleasure trips

   5 (b) came in or between in order to stop, settle, or modify something

   1 (c) a startling experience which has a lasting emotional effect; a shock

   3 (d) a contagious, sometimes fatal disease that produces a toxin causing inflammation of the heart and nervous system

   2 (e) a complex disease due to the excessive or compulsive consumption of alcohol often leading to a complex chronic psychological and nutritional disorder

Answer questions in complete sentences

1. <u>Why should Eleanor be remembered?</u>

   Eleanor helped people during her adult life promoting civil rights, social justice, and national unity. She was the eyes, ears, and legs for her husband during his political years after he was stricken with polio. Eleanor wrote a newspaper column. She wrote several books. She also chaired the committee that drafted the United Nations Universal Declaration of Human Rights.

2. <u>What traumas and unhappiness did Eleanor endure as a child and teenager?</u>

   Eleanor was frightened by the long drop into the rescue boat from a sinking ship as a toddler. Her mother, little brother, and father died when she was a little girl. After that, Eleanor lived with her strict grandmother, who would not allow her to attend college.

3. <u>How did Eleanor channel her interests and energies after she was denied the opportunity to attend college?</u>

   Eleanor worked at a settlement house helping immigrants and became a strong advocate for positive social change.

4. <u>Why did Eleanor become known as the First Lady of the World?</u>

   Eleanor was well-known around the world during her husband's long presidency because she traveled so much to help him. She chaired the committee that drafted the Universal Declaration of Human Rights for the United Nations.

Annie Sullivan

Match vocabulary words with definitions

1. meager

2. chronic

3. emulate

4. governess

5. valedictorian

3 (a) to imitate with effort to equal or surpass

2 (b) having a long duration and frequent recurrence

4 (c) a woman employed to take charge of a child's education and upbringing

1 (d) poor, inadequate, deficient in amount

5 (e) a student, usually the one ranking academically highest in the graduating class, who also delivers the farewell speech at the graduation ceremony

Answer questions in complete sentences

1. Why should Annie Sullivan be remembered?

Annie overcame many obstacles such as the loss of her family while very young, a chronic eye disease that damaged much of her vision, living in a bleak poorhouse, not attending school until late childhood, learning to read and write with Braille and manual alphabet systems, and as an adult teaching a deaf, blind, and mute child to communicate and succeed in earning a college education.

2. <u>What traumas in her childhood helped shape Annie's personal strengths?</u>

Annie lost her parents and brother early in life. She had no family to love and care for her. Annie was a sad, lonely child with vision problems. Annie threw tantrums out of frustration. She wanted to attend school, but it was a long time before anyone helped that happen. Annie learned to trust her kind teacher, Miss Moore, and overcame her frustration. Annie learned to keep trying until she succeeded.

3. <u>Why was Annie well-suited to be Helen's teacher?</u>

Annie had been a lonely and frustrated child with vision problems also. She could relate to how Helen felt. Annie realized that Helen had learned to throw tantrums when frustrated just as Annie had as a child. She knew that Helen would need to trust her in order to learn, just as Annie had come to trust Miss Moore. Annie knew how to teach Helen the Braille and manual alphabet systems to communicate.

4. <u>What evidence shows that Annie was modest about her own accomplishments in teaching Helen?</u>

Annie shied away from interviews and gave all the credit for Helen's learning to Helen.

Margaret Thatcher

Match vocabulary words with definitions

1. socialism
2. campaign

3. double standard

4. prime minister

5. persuade

2 (a) a series of planned actions undertaken to elect a candidate

4 (b) the chief executive of a parliamentary government (similar in duties and power to our president)

5 (c) to influence by argument or by asking earnest or urgent questions to bring someone to a belief or course of action

3 (d) a set of principles that apply differently and usually more vigorously to one group of people or circumstances than to another

1 (e) a form of government advocating collective or governmental ownership and administration of the means of production (in direct opposition to democracy and free enterprise)

Answer questions in complete sentences

1. <u>Why should Margaret Thatcher be remembered?</u>

She served as a member of Parliament and was the first, and so far, only female PM of Great Britain. Margaret wrote three books about politics and explained her view on democratic freedoms and free enterprise. She was America's and President Ronald Reagan's best ally from the 1980s onward.

2. Why do you think Margaret took her education so seriously?

Her father valued education but had been unable to attend college because he had to help his parents support their large family. As Margaret said, her father was a strong influence in her life. Her parents worked hard so Margaret and her sister could attend good private schools. Margaret was very interested in politics and felt she needed a law school education to succeed in politics.

3. Why do you think Margaret decided to run for prime minister?

From her work in Parliament, Margaret came to believe that socialism was not working. She believed it was actually making life worse for the British people, so she ran on the platform to abandon socialism.

4. Margaret said that her father was the biggest influence in her life. Who has been most influential in your life? How has that person helped you?

Answers will vary.

Harriet Tubman

Match vocabulary words with definitions

1. appease
2. scrawny
3. disoriented
4. liberator

5. underground railroad

   2 (a) extremely lean, skinny, or puny

   4 (b) a person who frees others from bondage

   5 (c) a system of cooperation and safe houses among active antislavery people who before and during the American Civil War helped enslaved people reach freedom in the North

   3 (d) confused; cause to lose bearings or sense of location or identity

   1 (e) pacify, calm, or cause to subside

Answer questions in complete sentences

1. <u>Why should Harriet Tubman be remembered?</u>

   Harriet helped hundreds of slaves escape to free Northern states. She fought for women's right to vote. She helped create schools for black students. Harriet's home was open to anyone in need. She appreciated the importance of freedom. Harriet was a Christian who appreciated her blessings and lived by her Christian beliefs.

2. <u>How did Harriet use an injury to benefit herself?</u>

   Harriet often faked disorientation and confusion from her head injury so that her slave owner would not be able to sell her to another owner who would take her away from her family.

3. <u>How did Harriet help so many slaves escape to freedom?</u>

Harriet secretly sneaked them out through the underground railroad system. Because she was a small female, no one suspected Harriet.

4. <u>What evidence is there that Harriet was thankful for her blessings?</u>

Harriet did not stay in the North after escaping the first time. She continued putting her own freedom and life at risk by returning again and again to the South to help others escape. Harriet fought for women's right to vote, set up schools for black children, and helped anyone in need.

Edith Wilson

Match vocabulary words with definitions

1. extravagance
2. compatible
3. privy
4. astute
5. widow

   4 (a) clever, ingenious, or keenly discerning

   3 (b) personal, secret, private; admitted as one sharing in a secret

   1 (c) wasteful, costly, or unwise expense

   2 (d) able to exist or act together harmoniously

5 (e) a woman who has lost her husband by death and has not remarried

Answer questions in complete sentences

1. <u>Why should Edith Wilson be remembered?</u>

    Edith continued to read and learn even after she had to leave school so her family could afford to educate her brothers. She was hardworking and resourceful, becoming a successful business owner after the death of her first husband. Edith supported her mother and siblings. She was a trusted advisor to her second husband, President Wilson. Edith could decipher secret enemy codes that had been intercepted during World War I. After the president suffered a stroke, she made important decisions while he was recovering.

2. <u>Why was Edith's formal education cut short?</u>

    Edith's family had little money and believed that it was more important to educate sons rather than daughters. It was a common belief that educating a daughter was an extravagance while educating a son was a necessity for a successful life.

3. <u>How did Edith meet Woodrow Wilson?</u>

    She met him while she was visiting her new friend, Helen Bones, the President's cousin who was sad about Woodrow's first wife dying. Edith's friend, Altrude Gordon, dated the White House physician, who suggested Edith and Helen become friends because they had so much in common. The doctor was worried about the grieving Helen.

4. How did Edith help her country during World War I?

She grazed sheep on the White House lawn, freeing the gardeners to do other work. Edith auctioned the sheep wool clippings for $100,000.00 and gave it to the Red Cross. She decoded secret enemy codes and was a trusted advisor to her husband.

Bibliography

Books

Adler, David. *A Picture Book of Eleanor Roosevelt*. New York: Holiday House, 1991.

Adler, David. *A Picture Book of Harriet Tubman*. New York: Holiday House, 1992.

Adler, David. *A Picture Book of Helen Keller*. New York: Holiday House, 1990.

Adler, David. *A Picture Book of Rosa Parks*. New York: Holiday House, 1993.

Allen, Paula Gunn and Patricia Clark Smith. *As Long as the River Flows, the Stories of Nine Native Americans*. New York: Scholastic, Inc., 1996.

Ashby, Ruth. *Rosa Parks, Courageous Citizen*. New York: Sterling Publishing, 2008.

Baines, Rae. *Harriet Tubman—The Road to Freedom*. New York: Troll Associates, 1997.

Bernstein, Richard B. and Jerome Agel. *Into the Third Century—The Supreme Court*. New York: Walker and Co., 1989.

Blackwell, Elizabeth. *Pioneer Work in Opening the Medical Profession to Women*. New York: Collectors Editions, 1970.

Bly, Nellie. *Around the World in 72 Days*. (Originally published New York: Pictorial Weekies. Now available at Twenty-First Century Books, 1999, and Kindle version at Amazon.com.)

Bly, Nellie. *Six Months in Mexico*. (Kindle version now available at Amazon.com.)

Bly, Nellie. *Ten Days in a Mad House*. (Originally published New York: Ian L. Munro, 1887, now available as paperback and Kindle version at Amazon.com.)

Brandt, Keith. *Marie Curie—Brave Scientist*. New York: Troll Associates, 1983.

Briad, Paul L. *Daughter of the Sky—The Story of Amelia Earhart*. New York: Harcourt, Brace and World, Inc., 1937.

Brownie Girl Scout Handbook. New York: Girl Scouts of the U.S.A., 2000.

Buchman, Dian Dincin. *Our 41st President—George Bush*. New York: Scholastic, Inc., 1989.

Bush, Barbara. *A Memoir*. New York: Charles Scribner's Sons, 1994.

Carawan, Guy and Candie. *Sing for Freedom—The Story of the Civil Rights Movement through Its Songs*. New South Books, 2008.

Caroli, Betty Boyd. *The First Ladies from Martha Washington to Laura Bush*. Garden City, New York: Guild America Books, 2001.

Clapp, Patricia. *Dr. Elizabeth—The Story of the First Woman Doctor*. New York: Lothrop, Lee and Shepard Co., 1974.

Cooney, Barbara. *Eleanor*. New York: Viking, 1996.

Cordery, Stacy A. *The Remarkable Founder of the Girl Scouts: Juliette Gordon Low.* New York: Scholastic, 2012.

Davidson, Mickie. *Helen Keller's Teacher.* New York: Four Winds Press, 1965.

Davis, Burke. *Lives to Remember: Amelia Earhart.* New York: G.P. Putnam's Sons, 1972.

Day, A. Grove. *Mark Twain's Letters from Hawaii.* New York: Appleton-Century, 1966.

Dunn, Andrew. *Marie Curie.* New York: Bookwright Press, 1991.

Earhart, Amelia (arranged by George P. Putnam). *Last Flight.* New York: Harcourt, Brace and World, Inc., 1937.

Earhart, Amelia. *The Fun of It.* New York: Harcourt, Brace and World, Inc., 1932.

Earhart, Amelia. *20 Hours, 40 Minutes—Our Flight in the Friendship.* New York: National Geographic Society, 2003.

Ferris, Jerri Chase. *Remember the Ladies—A Story about Abigail Adams.* Minneapolis: Carolhoda Books, Inc., 2001.

Gherman, Beverly. *Sandra Day O'Connor.* New York: Viking Press, 1991.

Giblin, James Cross. *Edith Wilson—The Woman Who Ran the United States.* New York: Viking Penguin, 1992.

Gormley, Beatrice. *Amelia Earhart—Young Aviator.* New York: Aladdin, 2000.

Guide for Daisy Girl Scouts. New York: Girl Scouts of U.S.A., 1986.

Hahn, Emily. *Around the World with Nellie Bly*. Boston: Houghton-Mifflin Co., 1959.

Hayes, Elinor Rice. *Those Extraordinary Blackwells*. New York: Harcourt, Brace and Co., 1967.

Heller, Ruth. *Fine Lines*. Katonah, New York: Richard C. Owen Publ., Inc., 1996.

Henry, Joanne Landers. *Elizabeth Blackwell—Girl Doctor*. New York: Aladdin Paperbacks, 1996.

Henry, Joanne Landers. *Marie Curie—Discoverer of Radium*. New York: MacMillan Co., 1966.

Heyn, Leah Lurie. *Challenge to Become a Doctor—The Story of Elizabeth Blackwell*. Baltimore: The Feminist Press, 1971.

Hintz, Martin. *Hawaii*. New York: Children's Press, 1999.

Hoyt, Helen. *The Princess Kaiulani*. North Island, Australia: Island Heritage, 1974.

Hughes, Libby. *Madame Prime Minister—A Biography of Margaret Thatcher*. Minneapolis: Dillion Press, 1989.

Hurtado, Albert L., editor. Mankiller, Wilma, introduction. *Reflections on American Indian History: Honoring the Past, Building a Future*. Norman: University of Oklahoma Press, 2008.

Jackson, Mahalia. *Mahalia Jackson Cooks Soul*. Nashville: Aurora Publ., Inc., 1970.

Jackson, Mahalia. *Movin' On Up*. New York: Hawthorne Books, 1966.

Jakes, John. *Great Women Reporters*. New York: G.P. Putnam's Sons, 1969.

Jones, Constance. *1001 Things Everyone Should Know about Women's History.* New York: Doubleday, 1998.

Jones, Victoria Garret. *Amelia Earhart—A Life in Flight.* New York: Sterling Publishing, 2009.

Johnson, Ann Donegan. *The Value of Caring—The Story of Eleanor Roosevelt.* La Jolla: Value Communications Publ., Inc., 1977.

Johnson, Ann Donegan. *The Value of Fairness—The Story of Nellie Bly.* La Jolla: Value Communications Publ., Inc., 1977.

Johnson, Ann Donegan. *The Value of Helping—The Story of Harriet Tubman.* La Jolla: Value Communications Publ., Inc., 1980.

Johnson, Ann Donegan. *The Value of Learning—The Story of Marie Curie.* La Jolla: Value Communications Publ., Inc., 1978.

Junior Girl Scouts Handbook. New York: Girl Scouts of the U.S.A., 2001.

Junor, Penny. *Margaret Thatcher: Wife, Mother, Politician.* London: Sidgwick and Jackson, 1983.

Kauger, Yvonne, Richard Du Bey, Wilma Mankiller, and Judy A . Zelio. *Promoting Effective State-Tribal Relations: A Dialogue.* National Conference of State Legislatures, 1990.

Klapthor, Margaret Brown. *The First Ladies.* Rev. ed. Washington D.C.: The Historical Association, 1989.

Krull, Kathleen. *Lives of Extraordinary Women.* San Diego: Harcourt, Inc., 2000.

Kudlinski, Kathleen. *Rosa Parks—Young Rebel.* New York: Aladdin Paperbacks, 1996.

Lauber, Patricia. *Lost Star—The Story of Amelia Earhart.* New York: Scholastic Inc., 1988.

Lepthien, Emilee. *The Cherokee.* Chicago: Chicago Press, 1985.

Long, Elgin M. and Marie K. Long. *Amelia Earhart— The Mystery Solved.* New York: Simon and Schuster Paperbacks, 1999.

Lovell, Mary S. *The Sound of Wings—The Life of Amelia Earhart.* New York: St. Martin's Press, 2009.

Mankiller, Wilma Pearl. *Mankiller: A Chief and Her People.* New York: Saint Martin's Press, 1999.

Mankiller, Wilma, Vine Deloria, Jr. and Gloria Steinem. *Every Day Is a Good Day: Reflections by Contemporary Indigenous Women.* Golden, CO: Fulcrum Publishing, 2004.

Mankiller, Wilma. *The Chief Cooks: Traditional Cherokee Recipes.* Muskogee, OK: Hoffman Printing Co., 1988.

Marks, Geoffrey and William K. Beatty. *Women in White.* New York: Charles Scribner's Sons, 1971.

McDearmon, Kay. *Mahalia—Gospel Singer.* New York: Dodd, Mead and Co., 1976.

McNeer, May and Lynd Ward. *Give Me Freedom.* New York: Abingdon Press, 1964.

Meigs, Cornelia. *Invincible Louisa.* Boston: Little, Brown and Co., 1968.

Meyer, Linda D. *Harriet Tubman—They Call Me Moses.* Seattle: Parenting Press, 1988.

Mrantz, Maxine. *Hawaii's Tragic Princess—The Girl Who Never Got to Rule.* Honolulu: Aloha Graphics and Sales, 1980.

Myerson, Joel and Donald Shealy. *Selected Letters of Louisa May Alcott.* 1987.

Nathan, Dorothy. *Women of Courage.* New York: Random House, 1964.

Parker, Robert Anderson. *The Great Jazz Artists.* New York: Four Winds Press, 1977.

Parks, Rosa. *My Story.* New York: Dial Books, 1992.

Radcliffe, Donnie. *Simply Barbara Bush.* New York: Warner Books, 1989.

Sabin, Francene. *Amelia Earhart—Adventure in the Sky.* New York: Troll Associates, 1997.

Sabin, Francene. *Young Eleanor Roosevelt.* New York: Troll Associates, 1997.

Sandak, Cass R. *The Franklin Roosevelts.* New York: Crestwood House, 1992.

Sandak, Cass R. *The George Bushes.* New York: Crestwood House, 1991.

Sandak, Cass R. *The Wilsons.* New York: Crestwood House, 1993.

Santrey, Lawrence. *Louisa May Alcott—Young Writer.* New York: Troll Associates, 1986.

Schwerin, Jules Victor. *Got to Tell It—Mahalia Jackson Queen of Gospel.* New York: Oxford University Press, 1992.

Scouting for Girls—Official Handbook of the Girl Scouts. New York: Girl Scouts of the U.S.A., 2011.

Seibert, Jerry. *Amelia Earhart, the First Lady of the Air.* Houghton Mifflin, 1960.

Simon, Charman. *Wilma P. Mankiller.* Chicago: Children's Press, 1991.

Smith, Barbara, Wilma Mankiller, Gwendolyn Mink, Marysa Navarro, and Gloria Steinem, editors. *A Reader's Companion to the History of Women in the U.S.* Boston: Mariner Books, 1999.

Stanley, Fay. *The Last Princess—The Story of Princess Kaiulani of Hawaii.* New York: Four Winds Press, 1991.

Steelesmith, Shari. *Elizabeth Blackwell—The Story of the First Woman Doctor.* Seattle: Parenting Press, 1987.

Steelesmith, Shari. *Juliette Gordon Low—Founder of the Girl Scouts.* Seattle: Parenting Press, 1990.

Stevenson, Robert Louis. *Travels in Hawaii.* Honolulu: University of Hawaii Press, 1973.

Thatcher, Margaret. *The Downing Years.* Harper Collins, 1993.

Thatcher, Margaret. *Statescraft.* Harper Collins, 2002.

Tobias, Tobi. *Marian Anderson.* New York: Thomas Y. Crowell Co., 1972.

Wagoner, Jean Brown. *Abigail Adams—Girl of Colonial Days.* New York: Aladdin Paperbacks, 1949.

White, Ellen Emerson. *The Royal Diaries—Kaiulani, the People's Princess.* New York: Scholastic Inc., 2001.

Witter, Evelyn. *Mahalia Jackson—Born to Sing Gospel Music.* Melford, Michigan: Mott Media Inc., 1985.

Zambucka, Kristin. *Princess Kaiulani of Hawaii: The Monarchy's Last Hope.* Honolulu, Hawaii: Mutual Publishing, 2005.

Articles

Asimov, Nannette. "Ruth Heller—Illustrator, Author of Children's Books." *SFGate* (July 3, 2004).

Barone, Michael. "A Woman in Full: Thatcher Gets Her Due in New Biography." *The Washington Examiner* (July 23, 2013).

Berss, Maria and Malcolm Forbes, Jr. "I Envy President Reagan." *Forbes* (July 28, 1986): 16.

Birdnow, Brian. "Dame Margaret Thatcher & the Heroine in History." *Townhall* (April 13, 2013).

Cunningham, Amy. "Good-Bye to Robin." *Texas Monthly* (February 1988).

Goodwin, J. "Tea with Margaret Thatcher." *Ladies Home Journal* (November 1987): 135.

Griffin, Rachel. "Black Herstory: Rosa Parks did Much More than Sit on a Bus." *MS. Blog* (February 3, 2012).

Hansen, Drew. "Mahalia Jackson and King's Improvisation." *New York Times* (August 27, 2013).

Hawkins, John. "In Tribute to the Iron Lady: The 25 Greatest Quotes from Margaret Thatcher." *Townhall Magazine* (April 9, 2013).

Jackson, Jesse L. "Appreciation: Rosa Parks." *Time Magazine* (October 30, 2005).

Keay, Douglas. "Margaret Thatcher's Life Story." *Good Housekeeping* (April 1985): 107.

Lawless, Jill and Cassandra Vinograd. "Britain's Iron Lady Laid to Rest with Full Pomp." *Associated Press* (April 17, 2013).

"Mahalia Jackson Included on Time Magazine's Top 100 Songs List." *Time Magazine* (October 25, 2011).

"Margaret Thatcher Opens Up on Her Life as a Woman, Wife, and World Leader." *People* (April 18, 1988): 28.

McFarland, "K. T." Katheen Troia. "Obama Snubs Thatcher Funeral." *Newsmax* (April 17, 2013).

Nelan, Bruce W. "Margaret Thatcher: A Legacy of Revolution." *Time Magazine* (December 3, 1990).

Patrick, Lisa. "Teaching Grammar Can Be Fun: An Oxymoron?" *Perspective Magazine* (May/June 2007).

Reed, David. "Maggie Thatcher: She's All Backbone." *Reader's Digest* (November 1987): 213.

Ruddy, Christopher. "Margaret Thatcher: The Final Word." *Newsmax* (May 2, 2013).

Sowell, Thomas. "Rosa Parks: Pursuit of Profit vs. Racism." *Capitalism Magazine* (October 27, 2005).

"Thatcher Takes on the Welfare State." *U.S. News & World Report* (June 17, 1985): 12.

"The Iron Lady Stands Alone." *Time* (April 26, 1986): 24.

Ward, Alexander. "Margaret Thatcher Dies: Social Media Reaction." *Newsmax* (April 8, 2013).

Interview

Jan Davis, correspondence interview by Sheryl Fearrien, February 11, 1997.

Websites

en.wikipedia.org/wiki/Abigail_Adams

en.wikipedia.org/wiki/Louisa_May_Alcott

en.wikipedia.org/wiki/Marian_Anderson

en.wikipedia.org/wiki/Elizabeth_Blackwell

en.wikipedia.org/wiki/Nellie_Bly

en.wikipedia.org/wiki/Barbara_Bush

en.wikipedia.org/wiki/Marie_Curie

en.wikipedia.org/wiki/Jan_Davis

en.wikipedia.org/wiki/Amelia_Earhart

en.wikipedia.org/wiki/Ruth_Heller

en.wikipedia.org/wiki/Mahalia_Jackson

en.wikipedia.org/wiki/Kaiulani

en.wikipedia.org/wiki/Juliette_Gordon_Low

en.wikipedia.org/wiki/Wilma_Mankiller

en.wikipedia.org/wiki/Sandra_Day_OConnor

en.wikipedia.org/wiki/Rosa_Parks

en.wikipedia.org/wiki/Eleanor_Roosevelt

en.wikipedia.org/wiki/Margaret_Thatcher

en.wikipedia.org/wiki/Harriet_Tubman

en.wikipedia.org/wiki/Annie_Sullivan

en.wikipedia.org/wiki/Edith_Wilson

www.abigailadams.com

www.louisamayalcott.org

www.mariananderson.org

www.elizabethblackwell.org

www.nelliebly.org

www.barbarabush.org

www.mariecurie.org

www.ameliaearhart.com

www.mahaliajackson.com

www.wilmamankiller.com

www.rosaparks.org

www.eleanorroosevelt.org

www.anniesullivan.com

www.margaretthatcher.org

www.harriettubman.com

www.harriettubman.org

www.edithwilson.com

www.aehof.eng.ua.edu/members/n-jan-davis

www.afb.org/asm/asbiography.asp (Annie Sullivan)

www.aip.org/history/curie/contents/htm (Marie Curie)

www.amazon.com?Ruth-Heller/e (her biography and books)

www.ameliaearhart.com/about/bio/html

www.ameliaearhart.museum.org/AmeliaEarhart/
AEBiography.htm

www.army.mil/article/98399 (Jan Davis)

www.barsbooks.com/Ruth%20Heller

www.biography.com/people/abigailadams

www.biography.com/people/louisamayalcott

www.biography.com/people/mariananderson

www.biography.com/people/elizabethblackwell

www.biography.com/people/nelliebly

www.biography.com/people/barbarabush

www.biography.com/people/mariecurie

www.biography.com/people/ameliaearhart

www.biography.com/people/juliettegordonlow

www.biography.com/people/wilmamankiller

www.biography.com/people/sandradayoconnor

www.biography.com/people/rosaparks

www.biography.com/people/eleanorroosevelt

www.biography.com/people/anniesullivan

www.biography.com/people/margaretthatcher

www.biography.com/people/harriettubman

www.biography.com/people/edithwilson

www.brainyquote.com/quotes/authors/m/marie_curie.html

www.brainyquote.com/quotes/authors/m/margaret_thatcher.html

www.csmonitor.com/Marie-Curie-why-her-papers-are-still-radioactive

www.distinguishedwomen.com (biographies of Abigail Adams, Louisa May Alcott, Marian Anderson, Elizabeth Blackwell, Nellie Bly, Barbara Bush, Marie Curie, Jan Davis, Amelia Earhart, Wilma Mankiller, Sandra Day O'Connor, Rosa Parks, Eleanor Roosevelt,

Annie Sullivan, Margaret Thatcher, Harriet Tubman, Edith Wilson, and many others)

www.findgrave.com/cgi-bin/fg.cgi?page=gr&GRid=535 (Mahalia Jackson)

www.firstladies.org/biographies (National First Ladies Library)

www.girlscouts.org

www.gos.sbc.edu/w/mankiller.html (Wilma Mankiller's 1993 speech: "Rebuilding the Cherokee Nation")

www.greatwomen.org/women-of-the-hall/search-the-hall-results/ (includes Abigail Adams, Louisa May Alcott, Marian Anderson, Elizabeth Blackwell, Nellie Bly, Amelia Earhart, Juliette Gordon Low, Wilma Mankiller, Sandra Day O'Connor, Rosa Parks, Eleanor Roosevelt, Annie Sullivan, and Harriet Tubman)

www.history.com/topics/abigailadams (articles, pictures, videos)

www.history.com/authors/harriettubman (articles, pictures, videos)

www.icivics.org (Sandra Day O'Connor's citizenship site for students and educators)

www.imdb.com/nm001730 (list of Louisa May Alcott's books and *Little Women* movies)

www.imdb.com/nm0413810 (Mahalia Jackson)

www.infoplease.com/encyclopedia/people/anderson-marian.html

www.jsc.nasa.gov/Bios/htmlbios/davis.html

www.kaiulani.freeservers.com

www.last.fm/music/Mahalia+Jackson-mn000814657

www.law.cornell.edu/supct/justices/oconnor.bio.html

www.mahaliajackson.us

www.mass.hist.org/digitaladams/aea/letter/ (correspondence between Abigail and John Adams)

www.math.buffalo.edu/~sww/Ohistory/hwny-tubman.html

www.nlm.nih.gov/changingthefaceofmedicine/physicians/
biography_35.html (Elizabeth Blackwell)

www.nwhp.org (National Women's History Project)

www.womenshistory.about.com (Good source of quota-
tions by Abigail Adams, Louisa May Alcott, Marian
Anderson, Elizabeth Blackwell, Barbara Bush, Marie
Curie, Amelia Earhart, Wilma Mankiller, Sandra Day
O'Connor, Rosa Parks, Eleanor Roosevelt, Margaret
Thatcher, Harriet Tubman, and many others. Also
good source of biographies for Abigail Adams, Louisa
May Alcott, Elizabeth Blackwell, Nellie Bly, Barbara
Bush, Marie Curie, Amelia Earhart, Wilma Mankiller,
Sandra Day O'Connor, Rosa Parks, Eleanor Roosevelt,
Margaret Thatcher, and Harriet Tubman.)

www.womeninworldhistory.com (Margaret Thatcher)

DVDs, Videos, Movies, YouTube Films

Abigail Adams

American Experience—*John & Abigail Adams* (TV Episode)
HBO Miniseries—*John Adams* (HBO Films, 2008)

Louisa May Alcott

Little Men (movie, 1934)

Little Women (movie, 1994)
The Inheritance (movie, 1997)
An Old Fashioned Thanksgiving (DVD, 2008)

Marian Anderson

Marian Anderson (movie, 1991)

Elizabeth Blackwell

The Blackwell Story (movie, 1957)

Nellie Bly

American Experience—*Around the World in 72 Days* (TV Episode)

Barbara Bush

History Channel—*The Wedding of George & Barbara Bush*

Marie Curie

Madame Curie (YouTube)

Jan Davis

N. Jan Davis '77 (YouTube)

Amelia Earhart

Biography—*Amelia Earhart—A Daring Pilot* (brief online video)
20th Century Fox—*Amelia* (DVD, 2009)

Mahalia Jackson

Mahalia Jackson (VHS, 1997)

Mahalia Jackson—The Power of Glory (VHS, 1998)

The Life and Music of the World's Greatest Gospel Singer (DVD, 2003)

Mahalia Jackson—Give God the Glory (DVD, 2004)

Mahalia Jackson Sings Songs of Christmas (DVD, 2005)

Jackson, Mahalia—The Immortal (DVD, 2006)

Mahalia Jackson 1957–1962 (DVD, 2007)

Mahalia Jackson: Got to Tell It (DVD, 2008)

Mahalia Jackson Sings (DVD, 2008)

Mahalia Jackson: You'll Never Walk Alone (DVD, 2008)

A Gospel Calling: Mahalia Jackson Sings (DVD, 2010)

Princess Victoria Kaiulani

Princess Kaiulani (DVD, 2010)

Long play record

Morrissey, Muriel Earhart. *Ameila Earhart, the First Woman to Fly the Atlantic Solo.* Anaheim: George Garabedian Productions. (Available at Humboldt State University, Arcata, CA 95521, HSU Library (Reference and Hours Open phone 1-707-826-3416)

CPSIA information can be obtained
at www.ICGtesting.com
Printed in the USA
LVOW04s0055221016

509645LV00011B/149/P